ENDORSEMENTS

"Are you in need of inspiration? Are you searching for a deeper faith and the strength to walk victoriously through challenging times? Then Dr. Eno Oton's *The Power of Courageous Faith* will bless and strengthen you.

This book offers a timeless and timely message: Even when we can't see it, God is always working behind the scenes for our good. Dr. Oton's inspiring words will uplift your spirit and equip you with the courage to face any obstacle with unwavering faith."

—Dr. Patricia King
Author, Minister, Media Producer and Host

"Dr. Eno Oton wrote *The Power of Courageous Faith* to share her personal journey and relatable challenges moving from her home in Nigeria to the United States. As she endeavored to remain faithful to her faith in God and allow her steps to be ordered by God, she uncovered the immense benefits of prayer.

Her stories of overcoming personal challenges, escaping danger, and praying for friends share both the love of God and practical ways to access the power of God. Praying Scriptures, feasting on God's Word, fasting, generosity, and other spiritual disciplines are a sincere call to a personal relationship with Jesus Christ."

—Michele Jackson
Senior Pastor, Hope Christian Church

"Dr. Eno Oton's book on the impact of prayer and miracles in her personal life are amazing and compelling. She not only shares how God met her with His miraculous presence in moments of crisis and everyday life, but Dr. Oton also lays out a course on how you can declare and activate your faith. Prepare your heart to receive all that God has abundantly in store for you!"

—Dr. David C. Parlette
Pastor, Hope Christian Church

THE
POWER
OF
COURAGEOUS
FAITH

GOD IS WORKING FOR YOU
BEHIND THE SCENES

THE
POWER
OF
COURAGEOUS
FAITH

DR. ENO OTON

Copyright © 2024 by Dr. Eno Oton

All rights reserved.

No part of this book may be reproduced in any form or by any electronic or mechanical means, including information storage and retrieval systems, without written permission from the author, except for the use of brief quotations in a book review.

Scripture quotations marked "KJV" are taken from the Holy Bible, King James Version (Public Domain).

Scripture quotations marked (NKJV) are taken from the New King James Version®. Copyright © 1982 by Thomas Nelson. Used by permission. All rights reserved.

ISBN Paperback: 978-1-961557-52-9

ISBN Ebook: 978-1-961557-53-6

Library of Congress Control Number: 9781961557529

Messenger Books
30 N. Gould Ste. R
Sheridan, WY 82801

CONTENTS

Endorsements	1
Foreword	11
Introduction	13
1. The Power of Prayer	15
2. Miracle Working God	25
3. Know God's Word for Wisdom and Revelation	36
4. Praying the Word of God with Wisdom	47
5. Your Inheritance and Positional Advantage in Christ	59
6. Praying for the Will of God	70
7. Weapons of Warfare: Praise, Thanksgiving, and Worship	81
8. When You Make a Vow to the Lord, Follow Through	92
9. Finding Peace in Any Situation	103
10. What Is Fear?	114
11. Deliverance from the Enemy	126
12. Where Is God When Things Are Going Wrong?	140
13. God Is a Story Changer	151
14. The God of Restoration	163
15. The God of the Eleventh Hour	174
16. Final Thoughts	184
Notes	189
Acknowledgments	191
About the Author	193

I dedicate this book to my son, Etikoh. Thank you for providing peace, love, and support. This book could not have been written without you.

FOREWORD

The world can be a tempestuous place. Headlines scream of turmoil, personal struggles loom large, and doubt can easily creep in, whispering that hope is a fragile thing. It's in these very moments, when the winds of adversity howl, that faith becomes our most vital anchor.

Dr. Eno Oton's book, *The Power of Courageous Faith,* is not a promise of a trouble-free life. It is, however, a beacon of light, a testament to the enduring power of faith in the face of hardship. Within these pages, you'll find stories of resilience, wisdom gleaned from the depths of struggle, and practical guidance for nurturing your faith when the going gets tough.

For anyone in a battle for faith, this book is a must-read. It offers real-life stories, actionable advice, and a powerful message of hope that will help you find strength and perseverance. God's Word is held up as the source of life and peace to anchor the soul through any storm life brings, whether that be job loss, illness, grief, or relationship problems. Eno will encourage you with the timeless truth that nothing is impossible for God.

Whether you're a seasoned believer seeking renewed strength or someone just starting to explore the concept of faith, this book offers something for you. It reminds us that we are not alone in our struggles, that God walks beside us, and that even in the darkest of nights, the dawn will come. Until that moment when light breaks in, the powerful light of God's Word illuminates our way and gives us real strength and lasting peace.

So, open this book with an open heart. Receive Eno's loving and expert guidance, and let her godly counsel from the truth of the Bible be a balm for your worries, a spark for your hope, and a reminder of the unwavering strength of Christ, who dwells in you and fuels your faith from trial to triumph.

—Teresa Yancy
Founder, Unlocking Your Book
Author, *Unveiled by God* and *The Messenger Life*

INTRODUCTION

Are you going through hell on earth? Be encouraged. There is hope for you. Do not forget that God Most High rules over the affairs of men. This book will help enrich your spiritual and physical life. If you cry yourself to sleep most nights, the Prince of Peace can give you enduring peace. The goal is to connect you to Him because He has answers to your difficult questions. Trust Him. He remains faithful to His Word.

In addition, this book will empower and encourage you to develop a personal relationship with the Savior. The testimonies in this book will stir up godly jealousy in you. God knew you before you were born. He knows your end from your beginning. This book is in your hands because the Lord wants to unveil the beautiful life He has prepared for you before you depart. Living in this hectic world in peace is possible because the Lord says so. Take Him at His Word, trust, and obey. Why? Because obedience is better than sacrifice. Call upon Him, pray, and seek Him. He promised:

For I know the thoughts that I think toward you, saith the Lord, thoughts of peace, and not of evil, to give you an expected end. Then shall ye call upon me, and ye shall go and pray unto me, and I will hearken unto you. And ye shall seek me and find me when ye shall search for me with all your heart."

JEREMIAH 29:11–13, KJV

May the Holy Ghost empower you to receive answers to your difficult questions and experiences in the wonderful name of our Lord and Savior, Jesus Christ. Amen.

ONE
THE POWER OF PRAYER

*"Likewise, the Spirit also helpeth our infirmities:
for we know not what we should pray for as we ought:
but the Spirit itself maketh intercession for us
with groanings which cannot be uttered."*
—**Romans 8:26, KJV**—

Prayer is so important that God commands us to pray always: *"And he spake a parable unto them to this end, that men ought always to pray, and not to faint"* (Luke 18:1, KJV). Prayer is a system of growth and transformation. It draws you closer to the Lord and helps you develop fellowship with Him.

Because we can only communicate with the Lord through prayer, the enemy will place obstacles in the way to block us from praying. The enemy does not want you to pray. Invite the Holy Spirit to help you. When you do, He will bring Heaven's power into your life.

PRAYER IS POWERFUL

Before I left Nigeria for the United States, I prayed and was confident in God's promise that I would not be jobless. God kept His word and has continued to keep it. I have not been without a job since I moved in 1985. He has opened the windows of Heaven, and He has blessed me abundantly, just as He promised in Malachi 3:10 (KJV):

> *Bring ye all the tithes into the storehouse, that there may be meat in mine house, and prove me now herewith, saith the Lord of hosts, if I will not open you the windows of heaven, and pour you out a blessing, that there shall not be room enough to receive it."*

When you tithe, you allow the blessings of the Lord to flow into your life. You replace the curses of not tithing with the blessings of tithing: *"Will a man rob God? Yet ye have robbed me. But ye say, wherein have we robbed thee? In tithes and offerings. Ye are cursed with a curse: for ye have robbed me, even this whole nation"* (Malachi 3:8–9, KJV).

In addition, the Lord promises this when you tithe: *"And I will rebuke the devourer for your sakes, and he shall not destroy the fruits of your ground; neither shall your vine cast her fruit before the time in the field, saith the Lord of hosts. And all nations shall call you blessed: for ye shall be a delightsome land, saith the Lord of hosts"* (Malachi 3:11–12, KJV).

When I pray, I pray the Word back to the Lord, reminding Him of what He said—because He said that I could do it! He stated, *"Put me in remembrance: let us plead together: declare thou, that thou mayest be justified"* (Isaiah 43:26, KJV).

I put God in remembrance of His Word every day of my life. Child of God, please pray because prayer works. Even when the enemy wants you to believe your prayer is going unanswered, continue to pray.

Remember these words from the apostle Paul: *"We walk by faith, not by sight"* (2 Corinthians 5:7, KJV).

I am a living witness, and I can attest that prayer is powerful. In addition to praying, you must also praise, worship, read, and study the Word of God. These spiritual activities are your lifeline. They are vital to your growth and development in spiritual affairs.

PRAYER AND FASTING

Life is spiritual. According to 2 Corinthians 4:18 (KJV), *"While we look not at the things which are seen, but at the things which are not seen: for the things which are seen are temporal; but the things which are not seen are eternal."* You must live a life of prayer in addition to living a life that pleases Father God. I recommend fasting and praying a day or two every week to wait on the Lord. Jesus fasted and prayed. Who are you emulating? The disciples of Jesus once asked Jesus why they could not cast out the lunatic spirit from the boy. Jesus replied, *"Howbeit this kind goeth not out but by prayer and fasting"* (Matthew 17:21, KJV).

If you have medical conditions, consult with your doctor before fasting. For prayer, you do not need permission from anyone. Pray as the Lord gives you the ability to. It is the Word of God: *"Pray without ceasing"* (1 Thessalonians 5:17, KJV).

MY ENCOUNTERS WITH THE SPIRIT OF DEATH

When I was in high school, I lived in a dormitory. On my way to visit my parents, I had a terrible experience at sea. On select weekends, students were permitted to visit their hometowns or families. For me, the access from the dormitory to my village was through a bridge in a car. This route was far away. The other way was to cross over to a nearby town called Ukan in a canoe, which was one village away from my own. The name of my village is Ikot Ndien, in Edem Aya, Ikot Abasi, Nigeria.

It was a lovely day. It was close to sunset, and because the weather was comfortable, I took a canoe to go home. Usually, three to six passengers can be in a canoe. On this particular day, though, it was just me and the gentleman who paddled the canoe. I was glad he pulled up at the shore to give me a ride because the evening drew close. There were no other passengers, so we started the journey.

When we got to the middle of the sea, the man had a seizure. There was no one around us, and I was helpless. I did the only thing I knew how to do: I prayed. I called upon the God my father introduced me to in Psalm 121. God, who is rich in mercy, came to my rescue.

As I prayed, I sat and watched the canoe propel itself to the shore. All glory to God. According to His Word, God helps those who are in trouble:

 God is our refuge and strength, a very present help in trouble. Therefore, will not we fear, though the earth be removed, and though the mountains be carried into the midst of the sea. Though the waters thereof roar and be troubled, though the mountains shake with the swelling thereof. Selah. There is a river, the streams whereof shall make glad the city of God, the holy place of the tabernacles of the most High. God is in the midst of her; she shall not be moved: God shall help her, and that right early."

PSALM 46:1–5, KJV

The power of prayer miraculously saved me. Although the captain had a seizure, God prevented the canoe from capsizing. The Almighty God, the Captain of the sea, took over the journey. I arrived safely on the other side. I give God all the glory for preserving my life and the life of the man onboard. Each time I remember this incident, my eyes get teary.

What storm are you experiencing in your life? The Lord Jesus is in control. Invite Him to help you handle the problems that currently afflict you. I found myself in trouble in the middle of the sea; with no physical help, I called upon God, and He answered me. He showed up and delivered me from the power of death. I am alive to tell the story. What a great testimony of God's faithfulness. He will do the same for you if you call upon Him in your time of trouble. Fear not. Believe that He can do what He promised. When His disciples were helpless at sea, they called Him for help. He helped them, as indicated in the following biblical narrative:

> *And there arose a great storm of wind, and the waves beat into the ship, so that it was now full. And he was in the hinder part of the ship, asleep on a pillow: and they awake him, and say unto him, Master, carest thou not that we perish? And he arose, and rebuked the wind, and said unto the sea, Peace, be still. And the wind ceased, and there was a great calm. And he said unto them, why are ye so fearful? How is it that ye have no faith?"*
>
> MARK 4:37–40, KJV

For me, there was also a great calm. I cannot imagine what the disciples felt when confronted by that terrible storm on their way to the other side. The Lord showed up for me, took charge of the situation, and gave me great peace. What the enemy meant for evil, look at God using it now for His glory.

My faith in God became stronger because of my experience at sea. When the situation became hopeless, the God of Heaven and earth came to my rescue. I believe there is a God in Heaven who answers prayer.

From my multiple experiences with the troubles of this world, I have learned that God shows up and miraculously turns situations around. I am amazed at His love for me. In any dilemma you may face, you can trust God, pray, and call upon Him.

MY SECOND ENCOUNTER WITH THE SPIRIT OF DEATH

When I moved from Nigeria to the USA, I settled in Raleigh, North Carolina. I worked at a Wendy's fast-food restaurant in a town called Cary. One night, I was leaving the store around midnight. An employee came with me to the door to lock it behind me. But when I opened the door to leave the store, a gunman was standing there.

The gunman took me hostage, held the weapon to my neck, and told the employee who came with me to the door, "I will kill her if you lock the door." But my coworker was too frightened. She locked the door and ran to the back of the store. I was left alone outside with the gunman.

Again, I went into prayer mode. God gave me the spirit of boldness, and I started praying in the spirit and quoting Scriptures. The gunman saw something I did not see while I was praying in the spirit. He let go of my neck and fled into the nearby bushes. The Word of God describes why the gunman reacted as he did:

 The Lord shall cause thine enemies that rise up against thee to be smitten before thy face: they shall come out against thee one way and flee before thee seven ways."

DEUTERONOMY 28:7, KJV

I continued to pray in the spirit, praising the Lord. It took a while for the police to arrive, but God took care of the situation. I can't help but praise the Lord for His faithfulness to me. The Word of God is accurate. God delivered me from the terror by night.

> *Surely, he shall deliver thee from the snare of the fowler, and from the noisome pestilence. He shall cover thee with his feathers, and under his wings shalt thou trust: his truth shall be thy shield and buckler. Thou shalt not be afraid for the terror by night; nor for the arrow that flieth by day."*
>
> PSALM 91:3–5, KJV

We see a story in Scripture that shows the power of prayer. Jesus was hungry and saw a fig tree. But it was not time for the fig tree to produce fruit. When Jesus got to the fig tree and found no figs, He said a prayer, and God answered Him: *"And Jesus answered and said unto it, No man eat fruit of thee hereafter for ever. And his disciples heard it"* (Mark 11:14, KJV). The next day, while passing through, Peter said to Jesus that the fig tree He cursed was withered away:

> *And Jesus answering saith unto them, Have faith in God. For verily I say unto you, that whosoever shall say unto this mountain, be thou removed, and be thou cast into the sea; and shall not doubt in his heart but shall believe that those things which he saith shall come to pass; he shall have whatsoever he saith. Therefore, I say unto you, what things soever ye desire, when ye pray, believe that ye receive them, and ye shall have them."*
>
> MARK 11:22–24, KJV

TRUST GOD—HE KEEPS HIS WORD

The goal of this chapter is to encourage you to trust the Lord with all your heart, even in challenging situations. When you find yourself with your back against the wall, do not give up. Look up. God has answers to complex problems. He is the same God that delivered the children of Israel from the hands of their enslaver. And as indicated in His Word, nothing is too hard for Him: *"Ah Lord God! behold, thou hast made the heaven and the earth by thy great power and stretched out arm, and there is nothing too hard for thee"* (Jeremiah 32:17, KJV). Nothing is too complicated for God to handle. What mountain in your life has refused to move? With God, all things are possible. Speak to that mountain and command it to move in the name of Jesus, just as He taught: *"Therefore, I say unto you, what things soever ye desire, when ye pray, believe that ye receive them, and ye shall have them"* (Mark 11:23, KJV).

PRAYER LESSONS FROM MY DAD

The greatest gift my dad gave me as a little girl was teaching me how to pray and read the Word of God. Before I left for high school, my dad would wake me up early in the morning, take me to his room, and ask me to kneel. Then he would pray for me and ask me to repeat Psalm 121 after him:

> *I will lift up mine eyes unto the hills, from whence cometh my help. My help cometh from the Lord, which made heaven and earth. He will not suffer thy foot to be moved: he that keepeth thee will not slumber. Behold, he that keepeth Israel shall neither slumber nor sleep. The Lord is thy keeper: the Lord is thy shade upon thy right hand. The sun shall not smite thee by day, nor the moon by night. The Lord shall preserve thee from all evil: he shall preserve thy soul. The Lord shall preserve thy going out and thy coming in from this time forth, and even for evermore."*

PSALM 121:1–8, KJV

Three months before the track competition in elementary school, we started inter-house practices. I ran a hundred-meter race. During the practice months, no matter how hard I tried, I came in second place. But, on the final day of the competition, I decided to bring God into the picture. Just before it was time for me to compete, I went to a corner and said the Lord's prayer:

> *Our Father which art in heaven, Hallowed be thy name. Thy kingdom come, thy will be done in earth, as it is in heaven. Give us this day our daily bread. And forgive us our debts, as we forgive our debtors. And lead us not into temptation but deliver us from evil: For thine is the kingdom, and the power, and the glory, forever. Amen."*
>
> MATTHEW 6:9–13, KJV

In the middle of the race, the girl that always took first place during practice fell. I passed her and won. As a little girl in elementary school, that answered prayer spoke volumes to me. I trust, respect, and value the God who answers prayer. I pray even when I don't feel anything, and more often than not, He shows up with an answer. When I look back at my two encounters with the spirit of death and on all my answered prayers, I am amazed at the love that the Lord has for me. That is why I worship with all my heart. To God be all the glory for His faithfulness.

SUMMARY

There are no age limits for God to answer your prayers. God is not a respecter of persons; He honors His Word. I encourage you to seek the Lord and call upon Him while you can. According to His Word, we need to seek Him while He is near: *"Seek ye the Lord while he may be found, call ye upon him while he is near: Let the wicked forsake his way, and the unrighteous man his thoughts: and let him return unto the Lord, and he will have mercy upon him; and to our God, for he will abundantly pardon"* (Isaiah 55:6–7, KJV).

PRAYER

Father, thank You for giving me the grace to trust and believe in You. I pray that You will help me to develop a fellowship time with You. Lord, help me to be consistent with my prayer life. As I pray, I trust that You will give answers to my prayers.

DECLARATION OF FAITH

Lord, I choose to believe Your Word, which declares, *"For with God nothing shall be impossible"* (Luke 1:37, KJV).

ACTIVATION

- Ask God to give you a supernatural encounter and experience with the power of prayer.
- Ask God to show you one thing that you need to do now to release the power of prayer in your life today.
- Speak to your prayer life. Command the mountain in your life to become a plain. Ask the Lord to do something beautiful in your prayer life.
- Be still, and listen to what the Lord has to say to you. Write down what you hear.

TWO
MIRACLE WORKING GOD

> *"Verily I say unto you, If ye have faith as a grain of mustard seed, ye shall say unto this mountain, Remove hence to yonder place; and it shall remove; and nothing shall be impossible unto you."*
> —**Matthew 17:20, KJV**—

A miracle is a supernatural occurrence God serves to deliver us from the power of the enemy and show that He is in charge. A miracle is sometimes an unexplainable encounter from the Lord. We see this in His words when He said to Moses in the wilderness, *"I will have mercy on whom I will have mercy, and I will have compassion on whom I will have compassion"* (Romans 9:15, KJV).

The Lord sometimes reveals and confirms His love for people by performing miracles in their lives. A miracle draws us to discern and receive the love of God in obedience. Jesus had mercy and compassion when He entered the synagogue and saw a man with a withered hand. The Pharisees watched Him to see if He would heal him on the Sabbath day. Jesus did not let the Pharisees stop Him and performed a miracle:

> *And he saith unto the man which had the withered hand, Stand forth. And he saith unto them, is it lawful to do good on the sabbath days, or to do evil? to save life, or to kill? But they held their peace. And when he had looked round about on them with anger, being grieved for the hardness of their hearts, he saith unto the man, Stretch forth thine hand. And he stretched it out: and his hand was restored whole as the other."*
>
> MARK 3:3–5, KJV

My prayer partner, Maggie, was barren for eighteen years. The Lord visited, revealed, and confirmed His love for her by performing miracles in her life. As you read about her testimonies, may the Lord perform miracles in your life.

I encourage you to thank the Lord today in prayer for your miracle. He is a faithful Father. If He did it for my prayer partner, He can do it for you. Believe Him.

YES! GOD STILL PERFORMS MIRACLES

Jesus is the same yesterday, today, and forever. Miracles are real, and the Lord performs miracles to manifest His works. When Jesus opened the eyes of a man who was blind from his birth, His disciples had questions:

> *And his disciples asked him, saying, Master, who did sin, this man, or his parents, that he was born blind? Jesus*

> *answered, neither hath this man sinned, nor his parents: but that the works of God should be made manifest in him."*
>
> JOHN 9:2–3, KJV

God wants to bless you and glorify His name through the wonderful work He performs in your life. When you share your testimonies, people who do not believe in miracles may have a change of mind. When my prayer partner, Maggie, shares her story with women looking for the fruit of the womb, they become receptive and hopeful. Hearing her testimony strengthens their faith. On many occasions, the women previously called barren have become mothers because they dared to trust God and believe in His miracle-working power.

PRAYER IS THE FOUNDATION OF OUR RELATIONSHIP

Maggie and I started praying together after we learned we both knew and loved the Lord. When I met her, Maggie's husband was still in Nigeria. She was believing in God for her husband to get a visa. Together, we asked the Lord to make way for Maggie's husband to enter the country, and the Lord answered our prayer. All glory to God.

When I asked for her perspective, Maggie wrote:

> *My husband was overseas when I met my prayer partner, Dr. Eno Oton. We started to pray, and God answered our first prayer together. My husband got a visa to the USA. I already believed in the Lord Jesus Christ. When I met her, I was still ignorant of the Word. One day, Dr. Eno Oton and I were together. She told me something someone did to her and said, "Let's pray about it." When we started praying, I prayed for God not to forgive that*

person. But my prayer partner stopped me. She said we need to pray in love. That began my prayer life with my prayer partner. I also limited myself to reading only our daily bread, not the Bible. But she explained the importance of reading the raw Word of God, the Bible. So, I started reading the Word, and the Word of God has changed my life for the better.

We have been praying together for over thirty years. The following are some prayer points we prayed and believed God for together. I was childless for eighteen years. We prayed, and God blessed me with three beautiful children. Two of my children were sick with asthma. We prayed, and they got healed. I fractured my leg. We prayed, and I got healed. I can walk without experiencing pain. I had financial hardship, and we prayed. The Lord made a way. My basement flooded for almost five years. We prayed, and God provided the finances. He also gave the contractors wisdom for adequately locating and fixing the flood problem. Prayer works.

CHILDLESS FOR EIGHTEEN YEARS

Maggie was barren for eighteen years after marriage. She tried everything she could but to no avail. When we prayed and believed God for a visa for her husband, God answered, which built up our faith. After the permit was approved, we started praying for the fruit of the womb for Maggie. We prayed and trusted God. The Lord answered and gave her a beautiful baby girl. Yes, miracles still happen. God opened the womb of a woman who was labeled barren and fulfilled His Word:

> *He maketh the barren woman to keep house, and to be a joyful mother of children. Praise ye the Lord."*
>
> PSALM 113:9, KJV

With God, all things are possible. If you have any need, call upon the God of miracles and watch God come through for you. God still answers prayer. Do not hesitate to pray to God with your most profound and secret needs. He remains faithful and honors His word. Whatever your need is, the Lord can meet you there.

Jesus is a miracle worker. See how He performed a miracle at the pool of Bethesda:

> *Now there is at Jerusalem by the sheep market a pool, which is called in the Hebrew tongue Bethesda, having five porches. In these lay a great multitude of impotent folk, of blind, halt, withered, waiting for the moving of the water. For an angel went down at a certain season into the pool and troubled the water: whosoever then first after the troubling of the water stepped in was made whole of whatsoever disease he had. And a certain man was there, which had an infirmity thirty and eight years. When Jesus saw him lie, and knew that he had been now a long time in that case, he saith unto him, Wilt thou be made whole? The impotent man answered him, Sir, I have no man, when the water is troubled, to put me into the pool: but while I am coming, another steppeth down before me. Jesus saith unto him, Rise, take up thy bed, and walk. And immediately the man was made whole, and took up his bed, and walked: and on the same day was the sabbath."*
>
> JOHN 5:2–9, KJV

HEALED OF ASTHMA

After we discussed the importance of reading the Word daily, Maggie started praying the Word out loud. She reminded the Lord about His promises and what He said about healing for her children. She read and prayed the Word over her children. Even when she did not see any physical evidence, she trusted and believed in God. He honored her faith and healed her boys of asthma. Yes, miracles still happen. We return all the glory to the Lord. Hallelujah!

> *He sent his word, and healed them, and delivered them from their destruction. Oh, that men would praise the Lord for his goodness, and for his wonderful works to the children of men! And let them sacrifice the sacrifices of thanksgiving and declare his works with rejoicing."*
>
> PSALM 107:20–22, KJV

FRACTURED LEG HEALED

When Maggie fell and fractured her leg, I knew it was an attack from the enemy for harming the kingdom of darkness. We were praying the Word, praising and worshiping God, and consistently reading the Word. We knew the enemy did not like how we were seeking the Lord.

Following the fracture, we increased the time that we prayed, fasted, praised, and worshiped the Lord. While Maggie was healing, God surprised us with another miracle. After the surgery, I went with Maggie to her follow-up appointment. When the doctor opened the wound, the surgical site looked like bread soaked in water. For people in the medical field, this description of a post-surgical site is not encouraging at all. It looked as if it needed to be amputated.

We pressed in for healing, and God heard our prayers. After the surgical site healed, I shared with Maggie what the surgical site had looked like, the potential for severe infection, and what could have happened had there not been a divine intervention by the Almighty God.

We thank God for our church, which encourages us to seek the Lord in prayer, praise, word, and worship.¹ That was what we did. Hallelujah! After the miracle physically manifested, I shared with Maggie the condition of the surgical site. Miraculously, there was no infection. How? Only the God who does mysterious and great acts can answer that question. We are careful to give God all the glory because He promised Maggie, *"For I will restore health unto thee, and I will heal thee of thy wounds, saith the Lord"* (Jeremiah 30:17, KJV).

REMOVING THE ORTHOPEDIC PLATE

The Lord showed up again. In the middle of the COVID-19 pandemic, the surgeon insisted that the plate be removed from Maggie's leg to prevent infection. I accompanied her for the procedure. All glory to God, we did not get infected with COVID while in the hospital. And to God be all the glory again, the surgical site healed well with no infection. Jesus Christ is our healer:

> *But he was wounded for our transgressions, he was bruised for our iniquities: the chastisement of our peace was upon him; and with his stripes we are healed. All we like sheep have gone astray; we have turned everyone to his own way; and the Lord hath laid on him the iniquity of us all."*
>
> ISAIAH 53:5–6, KJV

GOD USES MIRACLES TO FIGHT FOR HIS PEOPLE

The Lord miraculously fought for the Israelites, the people He loves, by tearing down the wall of Jericho and giving them victory. God told Joshua that He had given into his hand Jericho, the king of Jericho, and the mighty men of valor. He instructed Joshua and his men of war to circle the city once a day for six days. In Joshua 6:4–5 (KJV), God commanded:

> *Seven priests shall bear before the ark seven trumpets of rams' horns: and the seventh day ye shall compass the city seven times, and the priests shall blow with the trumpets. And it shall come to pass, that when they make a long blast with the ram's horn, and when ye hear the sound of the trumpet, all the people shall shout with a great shout; and the wall of the city shall fall down flat, and the people shall ascend up every man straight before him."*

Miraculously, God showed up and fought for the children of Israel. He instructed the priests to take up the Ark of the Covenant and let seven priests bear seven trumpets of rams' horns before the ark of the Lord. Joshua commanded the people to pass on and compass the city of Jericho. In Joshua 6:7 (KJV), Joshua stated, *"and let him that is armed pass on before the ark of the Lord."* When they obeyed the Lord, the children of Israel had a great victory:

> *So, the people shouted when the priests blew with the trumpets: and it came to pass, when the people heard the sound of the trumpet, and the people shouted with a great shout, that the wall fell down flat, so that the people went up into the city, every man straight before him, and they took the city."*

JOSHUA 6:20, KJV

GOD USES MIRACLES TO CONFIRM HIS TRUE MESSENGERS

Elijah was a faithful messenger of God. King Ahaziah was sick and sent messengers to ask Baalzebub, the god of Ekron, whether he

THE POWER OF COURAGEOUS FAITH   33

would recover from this disease instead of inquiring from the God of Israel. The Lord was not pleased with the king. He asked Elijah to tell him he would die: *"Thus saith the Lord, is it not because there is not a God in Israel, that thou sendest to enquire of Baalzebub the god of Ekron? therefore thou shalt not come down from that bed on which thou art gone up, but shalt surely die"* (2 Kings 1:6, KJV).

King Ahaziah sent messengers to summon Elijah, asking him to come down from the hill. But Elijah called down fire to consume them: *"And Elijah answered and said to the captain of fifty, If I be a man of God, then let fire come down from heaven, and consume thee and thy fifty. And there came down fire from heaven and consumed him and his fifty"* (2 Kings 1:10, KJV). When you trust and believe in God, He will prove His Word.

When Jesus raised Lazarus from the dead, God confirmed that Jesus was His faithful messenger by demonstrating His power and proving His Word.

> *Then they took away the stone from the place where the dead was laid. And Jesus lifted up his eyes, and said, Father, I thank thee that thou hast heard me. And I knew that thou hearest me always: but because of the people which stand by I said it, that they may believe that thou hast sent me. And when he thus had spoken, he cried with a loud voice, Lazarus, come forth. And he that was dead came forth, bound hand and foot with graveclothes: and his face was bound about with a napkin. Jesus saith unto them, Loose him, and let him go."*
>
> JOHN 11:41–43, KJV

After Paul and those with him escaped from the island of Melita, a viper attacked Paul. But Paul shook off the viper into the fire and was not hurt. The people were amazed. By miraculously saving his life, God confirmed Paul to be His true messenger.

> *And when Paul had gathered a bundle of sticks, and laid them on the fire, there came a viper out of the heat, and fastened on his hand. And when the barbarians saw the venomous beast hang on his hand, they said among themselves, No doubt this man is a murderer, whom, though he hath escaped the sea, yet vengeance suffereth not to live. And he shook off the beast into the fire, and felt no harm. Howbeit they looked when he should have swollen, or fallen down dead suddenly: but after they had looked a great while, and saw no harm come to him, they changed their minds, and said that he was a god."*
>
> ACTS 28:3–6, KJV

SUMMARY

God is a good Father. He can perform miracles for you as He did for my prayer partner, Maggie. In addition, you read how the Lord miraculously fought for the Israelites, the people He loves, by tearing down the wall of Jericho and giving them victory. Allow these testimonies to build your faith and stir your heart to call upon the Lord. He will answer your call.

PRAYER

Lord, today I come to You. I trust in You and ask that just as You healed Maggie's children of asthma, You will restore and make me whole. And Lord, just as you blessed Maggie with the fruit of the womb, I pray that you meet me at the point of my need, which is _____ (insert your need). Lord, as I call upon You, the

God of miracles, I pray that You visit me with blessings and breakthroughs. In the name of Jesus, I pray. Amen.

DECLARATION OF FAITH

Lord, I believe that You will visit me and bless me with a miracle. I thank You for doing something beautiful in my life as I look up to You.

ACTIVATION

- Ask God to show you any area of your life where you need a miracle.
- Ask God to show you one thing you must do now to release a miracle in your life.
- Speak to any area in your life that needs a miracle. Command the mountain in your life to become a plain. Ask the Lord to do something beautiful in your life today.
- Be still, and listen to what the Lord has to say to you. Write down what you hear.

THREE
KNOW GOD'S WORD FOR WISDOM AND REVELATION

> *"Let the word of Christ dwell in you richly in all wisdom; teaching and admonishing one another in psalms and hymns and spiritual songs, singing with grace in your hearts to the Lord."*
> **—Colossians 3:16, KJV—**

The world as we know it is in chaos. It is a blessing to know that the Word of God has the solution to the mess we are facing. I give all the glory to God for not leaving us in the dark. God knows the end of all things from the beginning. He is the omnipotent, omniscient, and omnipresent One.

The Word of God communicates that we will have trouble in the world, but we are never without hope: *"These things I have spoken unto you, that in me ye might have peace. In the world ye shall have tribulation: but be of good cheer; I have overcome the world"* (John 16:33, KJV).

God's Word gives answers, insight, and encouragement. It provides peace to the troubled mind and illuminates the darkness of this world. This book confirms that God reveres His Word. We also should know, believe, and revere the Word of God.

Scripture calms the troubled soul. When you encounter trouble, God's wisdom can give you peace and advice. These are all documented in the Word of God for you to know. It is your responsibility to read, study, and apply the Word with wisdom to have a peaceful life. The following are some reasons to know God's Word for wisdom and revelation!

The Word of God Brings Purification

Isn't it encouraging and empowering to know that not all the sufferings that you encounter come as a result of sin? God trains us in preparation for the work He has called us to complete while on earth. Trials and tribulations train us for our assignments and keep us grounded, purified, and prepared for the task ahead for His glory.

The apostle Paul, who wrote the majority of the New Testament, encountered trouble while on earth. He revealed that God uses our unpleasant encounters to strengthen us.

And lest I should be exalted above measure through the abundance of the revelations, there was given to me a thorn in the flesh, the messenger of Satan to buffet me, lest I should be exalted above measure. For this thing I besought the Lord thrice, that it might depart from me. And he said unto me, my grace is sufficient for thee: for my strength is made perfect in weakness. Most gladly therefore will I rather glory in my infirmities, that the power of Christ may rest upon me."

2 CORINTHIANS 12:7–9, KJV

May the Lord grant you the grace to complete your assigned duties, even in the presence of adversity.

The Word Guides You to Seek the Lord

Seek the Lord and be prepared for whatever the enemy has planned for you. Remember, you don't have to do anything wrong to be visited by the enemy. The Bible encourages you to seek the Lord *before* you get into trouble. Often, people seek the Lord only when they are in danger or going through difficult times, but the Word of God encourages you to seek the Lord when He is near:

> *Seek ye the Lord while he may be found, call ye upon him while he is near. Let the wicked forsake his way, and the unrighteous man his thoughts: and let him return unto the Lord, and he will have mercy upon him; and to our God, for he will abundantly pardon."*
>
> ISAIAH 55:6–7, KJV

The Lord knows your end from your beginning. He sometimes allows situations in your life to cause you to seek Him for His purposes to be fulfilled. For example, for Hannah to birth one of the greatest prophets in Israel, she had to know how to seek and find God. Hannah's husband had two wives: Peninnah and Hannah. Peninnah had children, but God made Hannah barren. Hannah's barrenness forced her to seek God with all her heart. In addition, Peninnah, her adversary, mocked her.

Because Hannah knew the Word of God, she knew He could answer prayer. Hannah sought and wept before the Lord, pleading that He would give her a son. God answered her prayer and blessed her with Samuel, who later became a prophet. In addition, God blessed Hannah with five more children. Hannah was so appreciative that she wrote a song to the Lord, being careful to return the glory to God:

 And Hannah prayed, and said, my heart rejoiceth in the Lord, mine horn is exalted in the LORD: my mouth is enlarged over mine enemies because I rejoice in thy salvation. There is none holy as the LORD: for there is none beside thee: neither is there any rock like our God."

1 SAMUEL 2:1–2, KJV

What is it that the Lord asks you to lay down in your life? What is competing with God for your attention, preventing you from seeking Him? There is no shortcut to what the Lord is asking of you. You must willingly lay down what He is asking, sacrifice your time, and seek Him. Pray and ask God for the power to lay everything down.

Once you surrender what is holding you captive, you become free. You must submit your heart. Let Jesus be the center of your life. In the spirit realm, you gain by losing. Anything that you cannot afford to lose that is getting in the way between you and God is what Satan uses to accuse you before the Father. Seeking the Lord through His Word in wisdom and making a covenant with Him will change you for the better: *"Gather my saints together unto me; those that have made a covenant with me by sacrifice. And the heavens shall declare his righteousness: for God is judge himself. Selah"* (Psalm 50:5–6, KJV).

When you seek God and make a covenant through sacrifice, you receive rewards from the Lord. Abraham received a reward when he offered Isaac. What are you doing for the Lord? What are you afraid of losing? Ask the Lord to give you the grace to surrender the things that do not glorify Him.

You are a steward. All that you have belongs to Him. If you surrender all, He will be the One to maintain it all. If you don't, then you become the owner. As an owner, you carry the burden. Release it to the Lord. Change your status from owner to steward. Be a faithful steward:

> *Moreover, it is required in stewards that a man be found faithful."*
>
> 1 CORINTHIANS 4:2, KJV

The Word Helps You Comfort Others

Your pain sharpens your testimony. You learn how to be compassionate and show authentic empathy from personal experiences. Pain has a way of helping you relate to others who are experiencing the same thing. With wisdom from God's Word, use your pain to comfort others.

> *Blessed be God, even the Father of our Lord Jesus Christ, the Father of mercies, and the God of all comfort. Who comforteth us in all our tribulation, that we may be able to comfort them which are in any trouble, by the comfort wherewith we ourselves are comforted of God. For as the sufferings of Christ abound in us, so our consolation also aboundeth by Christ."*
>
> 2 CORINTHIANS 1:3–5, KJV

The Word of God Empowers You to Obey God

When the Israelites disobeyed God in the land of the Midianites, the Lord delivered them into the hand of Midian for seven years. The Midianites mistreated them and destroyed their property, including sheep, oxen, and donkeys. When the children of Israel cried to the Lord because of the Midianites' ill treatment, God answered their cry and sent an angel to Gideon, and with the Word of God, the children of Israel were delivered from the Midianites. However, Gideon had no confidence in himself, but God did: *"The angel of the Lord appeared unto Gideon and said unto him, The Lord is with thee, thou mighty man of valor"* (Judges 6:12, KJV).

The Lord asked Gideon to go and save his people from the Midianites. Although Gideon did not believe he could do it, the Lord, who knows the end of things from the beginning, did: *"And he said unto him, oh my Lord, wherewith shall I save Israel? behold, my family is poor in Manasseh, and I am the least in my father's house. And the Lord said unto him, surely, I will be with thee, and thou shalt smite the Midianites as one man"* (Judges 6:15–16, KJV).

Gideon agreed to do what the Lord had asked him to do, but he asked for a sign from the Lord. And the Lord, who is so gracious, gave him one:

> *And when Gideon was come, behold, there was a man that told a dream unto his fellow, and said, Behold, I dreamed a dream, and, lo, a cake of barley bread tumbled into the host of Midian, and came unto a tent, and smote it that it fell, and overturned it, that the tent lay along. And his fellow answered and said, this is nothing else save the sword of Gideon the son of Joash, a man of Israel: for into his hand hath God delivered Midian, and all the host. And it was so, when Gideon heard the telling of the dream, and the interpretation thereof, that he worshiped, and returned into the host of Israel, and said, arise; for the Lord hath delivered into your hand the host of Midian."*
>
> JUDGES 7:13–15, KJV

God empowered Gideon with the words spoken through a Midianite's dream. God can use anything to encourage and empower you to fulfill your assignment.

KNOW THE POWER OF YOUR WORDS

As you seek and get closer to God, be very careful with your words and what you allow to come out of your mouth. Think before you speak because the enemy can capture your comments and make your words work against you. He has been around for a very long time. He knows the power of words, and he also knows the Word of God. Satan is your enemy. If you allow it, know that Satan will stop at nothing to pervert God's Word and your own words. Listen to how the Bible describes the power of your words:

> *Thou shalt also decree a thing, and it shall be established unto thee: and the light shall shine upon thy ways. When men are cast down, then thou shalt say, there is lifting up; and he shall save the humble person."*
>
> JOB 22:28–29, KJV

THE SECRET OF THE LORD

The secret of the Lord for you is in God's Word. As you pray, read the Bible, and seek the Lord, He shows you what you need to know and the things that block you from moving forward in life. The following Scriptures confirm that the Lord is interested in helping you in your current troubled state. You must only find them and speak them over your life.

- *"The secret of the Lord is with them that fear him; and he will show them his covenant"* (Psalm 25:14, KJV).

- "Surely the Lord God will do nothing, but he revealeth his secret unto his servants the prophets" (Amos 3:7, KJV).
- "He that dwelleth in the secret place of the most High shall abide under the shadow of the Almighty" (Psalm 91:1, KJV).
- "For nothing is secret, that shall not be made manifest; neither anything hid, that shall not be known and come abroad" (Luke 8:17, KJV).

Are you troubled? Be encouraged. God is a revealer of secrets, and He can reveal the secret that will end the trouble in your life. Spend time seeking, praying, and talking to God, and remain in His presence. The more you draw closer to God, the more you get to know Him, and the more time you spend in His company, the more revelation you get from Him.

WISDOM AND REVELATION KNOWLEDGE

Seeking and attaining wisdom and revelation knowledge will help you make wise choices. According to Proverbs 11:30 (KJV), *"The fruit of the righteous is a tree of life; and he that winneth souls is wise."*

Wisdom and revelation knowledge can also help one share their experiences with people who may be going through the same thing. I pray for you *"that the God of our Lord Jesus Christ, the Father of glory, may give unto you the spirit of wisdom and revelation in the knowledge of him: The eyes of your understanding being enlightened; that ye may know what is the hope of his calling, and what the riches of the glory of his inheritance in the saints. And what is the exceeding greatness of his power to usward who believe, according to the working of his mighty power"* (Ephesians 1:17–19, KJV).

When you study the Word of God, you can increase in wisdom and receive favor: *"And Jesus increased in wisdom and stature, and in favor with God and man"* (Luke 2:52, KJV).

WHY YOU NEED WISDOM

Godly wisdom helps us to live a good quality life. The Bible states:

 Happy is the man that feedeth wisdom and the man that getteth understanding. For the merchandise of it is better than the merchandise of silver, and the gain thereof than fine gold. She is more precious than rubies: and all the things thou canst desire are not to be compared unto her. Length of days is in her right hand, and in her left-hand riches and honour. Her ways are ways of pleasantness, and all her paths are peace. She is a tree of life to them that lay hold upon her: and happy is everyone that retaineth her."

PROVERBS 3:13–18, KJV

In addition, we are told that *"wisdom is the principal thing; therefore, get wisdom: and with all thy getting get understanding. Exalt her, and she shall promote thee: she shall bring thee to honor, when thou dost embrace her. She shall give to thine head an ornament of grace: a crown of glory shall she deliver to thee. Hear, O my son, and receive my sayings; and the years of thy life shall be many"* (Proverbs 4:7–10, KJV). Therefore, wisdom is important because it provides you with the practical knowledge needed to navigate life.

My experiences with seeking God's wisdom and revelation knowledge has enriched my spiritual life in different ways. It can do the same for you. When you encounter problems, apply God's wisdom and revelation knowledge and see what happens.

WHY YOU NEED UNDERSTANDING

The Bible reveals the need for understanding God's Word. The following are a few of those key verses:

- *"And be not conformed to this world: but be ye transformed by the renewing of your mind, that ye may prove what is that good, and acceptable, and perfect, will of God"* (Romans 22:2, KJV).
- *"He that getteth wisdom loveth his own soul: he that keepeth understanding shall find good"* (Proverbs 19:8, KJV).
- *"Whoso is wise, and will observe these things, even they shall understand the lovingkindness of the Lord"* (Psalm 107:43, KJV).
- *"But let him that glorieth glory in this, that he understandeth and knoweth me, that I am the Lord which exercise lovingkindness, judgment, and righteousness, in the earth: for in these things I delight, saith the Lord"* (Jeremiah 9:24, KJV).
- *"The law of the Lord is perfect, converting the soul: the testimony of the Lord is sure, making wise the simple"* (Psalm 19:7, KJV).

You need understanding to help you navigate, establish, and live a godly life. A lack of understanding causes confusion. Having an understanding about something one needs to know helps one to make informed decisions about their choices.

SUMMARY

The Word of God gives answers, insight, and encouragement. It provides peace to the troubled mind. The Word of God illuminates the darkness of this world. It additionally reveals the impact of God's words and the power that accompanies the words that you speak.

PRAYER

Lord, please help build my house with wisdom and establish it with understanding. Lord, strengthen me as I gather knowledge, and help me watch the words that leave my mouth in Jesus's name. Amen.

DECLARATION OF FAITH

God's Word is my source of wisdom and revelation for life, ministry, and relationships.

ACTIVATION

- Know that the secret of the Lord for you is found in God's Word.
- Speak to the Lord, remind Him as you pray, read God's Word with wisdom, and seek the Lord to show you what you need to know about your life.
- Ask the Lord to show you the things that block your progress.
- Ask the Lord to reveal what is causing the delay in your request.
- Write down what you hear.

FOUR
PRAYING THE WORD OF GOD WITH WISDOM

"But we speak the wisdom of God in a mystery, even the hidden wisdom, which God ordained before the world unto our glory. Which none of the princes of this world knew: for had they known it, they would not have crucified the Lord of glory. But as it is written, Eye hath not seen, nor ear heard, neither have entered into the heart of man, the things which God hath prepared for them that love him. But God hath revealed them unto us by his spirit: for the spirit searcheth all things, yea, the deep things of God."
—**1 Corinthians 2:7–10, KJV**—

Praying the Word of God with wisdom allows Holy Spirit to reveal what we need to know from God the Father, God the Son (the Word), and God the Spirit. When you pray the Word of God with wisdom, it additionally builds your faith and trust in Him, making it easier to approach Him.

> *Now we have received, not the spirit of the world, but the spirit which is of God; that we might know the things that are freely given to us of God. Which things also we speak, not in the words which man's wisdom teacheth, but which the Holy Ghost teacheth; comparing spiritual things with spiritual."*
>
> 1 CORINTHIANS 2:12–13, KJV

Prayer is the time you set aside to fellowship and communicate with your Maker. You must be intentional about praying with wisdom. To pray with wisdom, you must familiarize yourself with the Word of God.

> *If ye abide in me, and my words abide in you, ye shall ask what ye will, and it shall be done unto you."*
>
> JOHN 15:7, KJV

Praying with wisdom includes knowing the Word of God, confessing the Word of God, supplication, praise, thanksgiving, adoration, and worship of God the Father, God the Son, and God the Holy Spirit. Praying with wisdom is when you pray God's Word back to Him, putting God in remembrance of His promises for you. Praying with wisdom is the time you approach God, ask, and petition Him for justification of your requests because He asked you to do so: *"Thus, saith the Lord, the Holy One of Israel, and his Maker, ask me of things to come concerning my sons, and concerning the work of my hands command ye me"* (Isaiah 45:11, KJV). The Lord encourages us in Isaiah 43:26 (KJV), *"Put me in remembrance: let us plead together: declare thou, that thou mayest be justified."*

JUSTIFICATION

Hezekiah prayed the Word of God with wisdom. Hezekiah was sick unto death. God sent the prophet Isaiah to go and tell him to set his house in order because he would die. If Hezekiah had not approached God with mercy and wisdom, he would have died. Because he applied the wisdom of God's Word to his prayer, though, God spared his life:

> *Then Hezekiah turned his face toward the wall and prayed unto the Lord. And said, remember now, O Lord, I beseech thee, how I have walked before thee in truth and with a perfect heart, and have done that which is good in thy sight. And Hezekiah wept sore. Then came the word of the Lord to Isaiah, saying. Go, and say to Hezekiah, thus saith the Lord, the God of David thy father, I have heard thy prayer, I have seen thy tears: behold, I will add unto thy days fifteen years."*
>
> ISAIAH 38:1–5, KJV

You can pray to God with wisdom and have your petition fulfilled. The Bible reveals that God cares for you, allowing you access to His Word. You are reading this book because the Lord wants you to continue or to start praying His words with wisdom.

> *Now all these things happened unto them for examples: and they are written for our admonition."*
>
> 1 CORINTHIANS 10:11, KJV

PRAYING THE WORD WITH WISDOM IS A WEAPON FOR SPIRITUAL WARFARE

To fight victoriously, you need the right kind of weapon. To use your weapon effectively, you must be in good shape, and to be in good condition, you must be prepared holistically. Your spiritual health depends on your holistic health. In other words, your mental and physical health have a direct affect on your prayer life.

> *For the weapons of our warfare are not carnal, but mighty through God to the pulling down of strong holds. Casting down imaginations, and every high thing that exalteth itself against the knowledge of God and bringing into captivity every thought to the obedience of Christ."*
>
> 2 CORINTHIANS 10:4–5, KJV

A practical prayer life equals glorious spiritual health. All warfare originates from the spirit realm and is empowered by strongholds. To engage appropriately and win in the spirit realm, you need a healthy spiritual life for the ongoing battle, which can only be obtained through praying the Word of God with wisdom:

The Equation: Mental Health + Physical Health + Praying the Word with Wisdom = Spiritual State

How would you like your spiritual well-being to look—victorious or defeated? Work on the equation, and remember that in the ongoing battle you face, using a spiritual weapon to fight is more effective than using a physical weapon. Praying the Word of God with wisdom is a more effective weapon than fighting in the natural.

The Bible states that we fight against wicked spirits: *"For we wrestle not against flesh and blood, but against principalities, against powers, against the rulers of the darkness of this world, against spiritual wickedness in high places"* (Ephesians 6:12, KJV). Therefore, to maintain a positive spiritual state, the Bible encourages that we persevere in prayer, *"praying always with all prayer and supplication in the Spirit and watching thereunto with all perseverance and supplication for all saints"* (Ephesians 6:18, KJV).

PRAYER AND OXYGEN

Prayer to the spirit is like oxygen to the physical man. When you fail to pray the Word of God with wisdom, your spirit gasps for life and is disconnected from the Creator. Just as you can die without oxygen, your spirit can die without prayer. Therefore, I believe you should pray the Word of God with wisdom. When you don't, you give the enemy access to destroy your life.

WHAT IS THE CONDITION OF YOUR PRAYER LIFE?

To have a healthy prayer life, praying the Word of God with wisdom is essential. How do you pray? At what time of the day do you pray? We often prioritize other things over praying, such as watching television, playing games, and talking on the phone. And, after all is said and done, we are tired, exhausted, and spent. I encourage you to set a specific time to spend with the Lord. It helps to set an alarm to remind and get you ready for your time with Him.

Self-Care

Praying the Word of God with wisdom reveals the will of God. It facilitates quality prayer time with your Maker. Do you know that self-care has much to do with your prayer life and time? It is crucial that you give your body the rest that it needs. If you notice that you feel tired quickly or frequently, talk to your doctor. If you have time to rest during the day, in preparation for quality prayer time at night before falling asleep, then you should.

Nourishment for Your Body

It is important that you make time to feed your body and eat healthy. When you are not fasting, you must plan to feed yourself nutritious meals to have the energy to complete your daily tasks, which includes praying the Word with wisdom. You cannot continue to run on empty all day and expect to have a good day or quality prayer time.

Sleep

You cannot stay up daily for long hours, binge television shows, or watch movies all night only to fall asleep while praying. If this happens to you frequently, it is time to make some changes. You need to prepare ahead of time to have quality prayer time. For example, if you fall asleep each time you get ready to pray, this is an indication that you need rest before your designated prayer time. It is important that you give your body enough sleep and rest.

Cell Phone

What about your cell phone? If a friend calls and asks if you are available to talk, do you stop praying and stay on the phone for hours with your friend? It is important that you do not use prayer time to talk or play around on the phone. There is no substitute for prayer.

So many factors are responsible for a good or a poor-quality prayer time that you must be aware of; you can only make changes if you are aware. I encourage you to pray the Word of God with awareness and wisdom. It will affect your prayer life positively.

LIVE PEACEABLY WITH ALL MEN

As much as you can, live a peaceful life with everyone. If you remember that you have anything against anyone, you should leave your offering and settle with that person:

Therefore, if thou bring thy gift to the altar, and there rememberest that thy brother hath ought against thee. Leave there thy gift before the altar and go thy way; first, be reconciled to thy brother, and then come and offer thy gift."

MATTHEW 5:23–24, KJV

Not everybody will like you. If you have tried multiple times to make amends with someone but they are unwilling, have peace. The Lord sees and knows your heart. The Lord knew His children would face opposition, so He addressed it. Be comforted by the Word of God. Pray it in love and with wisdom for those who despise you.

Recompense to no man evil for evil. Provide things honest in the sight of all men. If possible, as much as lieth in you, live peaceably with all men. Dearly beloved, avenge not yourselves, but rather give place unto wrath: for it is written, Vengeance is mine; I will repay, saith the Lord."

ROMANS 12:17–19, KJV

PRAY FOR ALL MEN AND RULERS

Praying the Word with wisdom helps us easily do what God asks us to do. The Lord commands that we pray for all men, including politicians that we may not like.

> *Therefore, I exhort first of all that supplications, prayers, intercessions, and giving of thanks be made for all men. For kings and all who are in authority, that we may lead a quiet and peaceable life in all godliness and reverence. For this is good and acceptable in the sight of God our Savior."*
>
> 1 TIMOTHY 2:1–3, KJV

When you pray the Word of God with wisdom, you allow the Spirit of God to direct you to those He wants you to reach out to for His glory.

> *Who will have all men to be saved, and to come unto the knowledge of the truth."*
>
> 1 TIMOTHY 2:4, KJV

SAMSON PRAYED THE WORD OF GOD WITH WISDOM

Even at the point of death, Samson prayed the Word with wisdom. As a result, he received answers to his prayers. From birth to death, Samson was a Nazarite. He fell in love and married a woman from the Philistines. The Lord planned to deal with the Philistines because they *"vexed and oppressed the children of Israel"* (Judges 10:8, KJV). Samson was mighty, and the Philistines asked his wife to ask Samson about the source of his strength. He did not reveal the basis of his power to his wife. He left, and Samson's wife was given to another man for marriage by her father. Then Samson met another woman. Still, he did not reveal the source of his strength. Finally, he met Delilah, and he loved her. She persuaded him to tell her where his power came from. He revealed that his hair was the source of his strength. The Philistines cut off Samson's hair and removed his eyes. To celebrate the capture of their enemy, the Philistines had a feast and offered a sacrifice to their god, Dagon. The Philistines made Samson perform for them in a banquet hall. But Samson's hair had begun to grow again, and his strength returned. Samson asked the person who held his hand to place him between the pillars that supported the hall, and when he did, he prayed:

> *And Samson called unto the Lord, and said, O Lord God, remember me, I pray thee, and strengthen me, I pray thee, only this once, O God, that I may be at once avenged of the Philistines for my two eyes. And Samson took hold of the two middle pillars upon which the house stood, and on which it was borne up, of the one with his right hand, and of the other with his left. And Samson said, let me die with the Philistines. And he bowed himself with all his might; and the house fell upon the Lords, and upon all the people that were therein. So, the dead which he slew at his death were more than they which he slew in his life."*

JUDGES 16:28–30, KJV

DANIEL PRAYED THE WORD OF GOD WITH WISDOM

Daniel became aware by reading the Word of God that it was time for the people of Israel to come out of captivity. He prayed the Word of God with wisdom:

> *And I prayed unto the Lord my God, and made my confession, and said, O Lord, the great and dreadful God, keeping the covenant and mercy to them that love him, and to them that keep his commandments."*

DANIEL 9:4, KJV

Daniel knew how to pray the Word of God with wisdom and receive answers:

> *Yea, whiles I was speaking in prayer, even the man Gabriel, whom I had seen in the vision at the beginning, being caused to fly swiftly, touched me about the time of the evening oblation. And he informed me, and talked with me, and said, O Daniel, I am now come forth to give thee skill and understanding. At the beginning of thy supplications the commandment came forth, and I am come to shew thee; for thou art greatly beloved: therefore, understand the matter, and consider the vision."*
>
> DANIEL 9:21–23, KJV

When you pray and ask God for anything, do not stop praying when you don't receive your petition on your timeline. The enemy might be blocking your answer. Daniel fasted and prayed for three weeks, but his prayer was delayed by principalities and powers. Thank God that Daniel did not stop praying. The angel of the Lord came to the rescue and delivered this word:

> *Then said he unto me, Fear not, Daniel: for from the first day that thou didst set thine heart to understand, and to chasten thyself before thy God, thy words were heard, and I am come for thy words. But the prince of the kingdom of Persia withstood me one and twenty days: but, lo, Michael, one of the chief princes, came to help me; and I remained there with the kings of Persia."*
>
> DANIEL 10:12–13, KJV

ESTHER PRAYED THE WORD OF GOD WITH WISDOM

Esther trusted God and prayed. When Mordecai perceived that Haman had approached King Ahasuerus, asking the king to destroy all the Jews for not keeping the king's laws, Mordecai rented his clothes, put on sackcloth with ashes, went out into the midst of the city, and cried with a loud and bitter cry. There was great mourning among the Jews. Many fasted, wept, wailed, and laid in sackcloth and ashes. Esther was made aware, and she sent a message to her uncle, Mordecai:

> *Go, gather together all the Jews that are present in Shushan, and fast ye for me, and neither eat nor drink three days, night, or day: I also and my maidens will fast likewise; and so, will I go in unto the king, which is not according to the law: and if I perish, I perish."*
>
> ESTHER 4:16, KJV

Esther found favor with her husband, King Ahasuerus, because she prayed the Word of God with wisdom. She invited her husband and Haman to the banquet of wine, where God showed mercy to the Jews.

> *And the king said unto Esther at the banquet of wine, what is thy petition? and it shall be granted thee: and what is thy request? even to the half of the kingdom it shall be performed."*
>
> ESTHER 5:6, KJV

SUMMARY

Before making any major decision, it is vital to pray the Word of God with wisdom for direction. Praying the Word of God with wisdom allows God to reveal what you need to know. Esther found favor with her husband, King Ahasuerus, and stopped the murder of Jews because she prayed the Word of God with wisdom. When you pray the Word of God with wisdom, just like Esther, fear disappears, and you can proceed with confidence to the throne room of God and receive your petition. According to 2 Timothy 1:7 (KJV), you become aware that fear is not your portion: *"For God hath not given us the spirit of fear; but of power, and of love, and of a sound mind."*

PRAYER

*Lord, I pray that You give me the grace to pray
Your Word with wisdom. I also ask that You
give me favor with You and with men.
In the name of Jesus, I pray. Amen.*

DECLARATION OF FAITH

I declare that my prayers are powerful when they are based on God's holy Word.

ACTIVATION

- Ask God to reveal to you how to pray His Word with wisdom.
- Ask God to show you what you need to change in your life as you pray His Word with wisdom.
- Write down what you hear.

FIVE
YOUR INHERITANCE AND POSITIONAL ADVANTAGE IN CHRIST

> *"That the God of our Lord Jesus Christ, the Father of glory, may give unto you the spirit of wisdom and revelation in the knowledge of him. The eyes of your understanding being enlightened; that ye may know what is the hope of his calling, and what the riches of the glory of his inheritance in the saints."*
> —**Ephesians 1:17–18, KJV**—

This chapter introduces you to your exalted position in Christ and reveals to you your positional advantage in Christ. According to Colossians 1:9 (KJV), Paul's prayer is that *"ye might be filled with the knowledge of his will in all wisdom and spiritual understanding."* Know that you have a position allocated just for you in the spirit realm, one that is important. Your place in the Lord reveals the riches of His inheritance and glory, giving you mental clarity and freedom from demonic spirits. Your position in Christ brings freedom and heals your spirit, soul, and body.

May the Lord help you to be spiritually minded: *"For to be carnally minded is death; but to be spiritually minded is life and peace. Because the carnal mind is enmity against God: for it is not subject to the law of God, neither indeed can be. So, then they that are in the flesh cannot please God"* (Romans 8:6–8, KJV).

As God's children, we have advantages that should be reflected in our lives. The finished work of Jesus on the cross gives us the audacity to live life with boldness and confidence: *"To the intent that now unto the principalities and powers in heavenly places might be known by the church the manifold wisdom of God. According to the eternal purpose which he purposed in Christ Jesus our Lord: In whom we have boldness and access with confidence by the faith of him"* (Ephesians 3:10, KJV).

Ignorance is dangerous, and you must educate and familiarize yourself with your rank in the spirit realm. The enemy does not want you to know or understand that you are seated in heavenly places in Christ Jesus, but you must know and understand it for it to be effective in your life.

> *But God, who is rich in mercy, for his great love wherewith he loved us. Even when we were dead in sins, hath quickened us together with Christ, (by grace ye are saved;) And hath raised us up together and made us sit together in heavenly places in Christ Jesus. That in the ages to come he might shew the exceeding riches of his grace in his kindness toward us through Christ Jesus."*
>
> EPHESIANS 2:5–7, KJV

Satan does not want you to know that God was satisfied by the travail of Jesus Christ's soul. This truth is powerfully revealed in Isaiah's prophetic words: *"He shall see of the travail of his soul, and shall* be satisfied: by his knowledge shall my righteous servant justify many; for he shall bear their iniquities" (Isaiah 53:11, KJV).

You have been justified. Jesus carried your sin. He paid in full the price for your iniquity. Just receive it. It is your gift.

THE LAW OF COMMANDMENTS IS SATISFIED BY CHRIST'S BLOOD

Jesus abolished the hostility caused by the law of commandments with His blood:

> *But now in Christ Jesus ye who sometimes were far off are made nigh by the blood of Christ. For he is our peace, who hath made both one, and hath broken down the middle wall of partition between us. Having abolished in his flesh the enmity, even the law of commandments contained in ordinances; for to make in himself of twain one new man, so making peace."*
>
> EPHESIANS 2:13–15, KJV

The enemy, the accuser of the brethren, cannot use ordinances to terrorize you anymore when you understand the love of God in the finished work of Jesus Christ:

> *Therefore, will I divide him a portion with the great, and he shall divide the spoil with the strong; because he hath poured out his soul unto death: and he was numbered with the transgressors; and he bare the sin of many and made intercession for the transgressors."*
>
> ISAIAH 53:12, KJV

In addition, Satan was cast down and can no longer accuse you:

> *For the accuser of our brethren is cast down, which accused them before our God day and night."*
>
> REVELATION 12:10, KJV

Jesus rescued humanity from the grips of Satan with His shed blood. He conquered Satan: *"And having spoiled principalities and powers, he made a shew of them openly, triumphing over them in it"* (Colossians 2:15, KJV). Jesus is in charge of all things, and you are complete in Him:

> *For in him dwelleth all the fulness of the Godhead bodily. And ye are complete in him, which is the head of all principality and power."*
>
> COLOSSIANS 2:9–10, KJV

The Almighty God has given you access to the Kingdom through the shed blood of Jesus Christ *"who hath delivered us from the power of darkness, and hath translated us into the kingdom of his dear Son. In whom we have redemption through his blood, even the forgiveness of sins"* (Colossians 1:13–14, KJV).

I pray that the Lord would open your spiritual eyes to see your positional advantage. Also, I pray for God to reveal your place in the Lord and the riches of His inheritance and glory: *"That Christ may dwell in your hearts by faith; that ye, being rooted and grounded in love. May be able to comprehend with all saints what is the breadth, and length, and depth, and height. And to know the love of Christ, which passeth knowledge, that ye might be filled with all the fulness of God"* (Ephesians 3:17–19, KJV). I pray also that you may know the matchless name of Jesus.

THE WONDERFUL NAME

There is no match in history to the name of Jesus. The name of Jesus is the universal key that can open every locked door. Simply put, Jesus Christ is Lord. As you follow Christ, let His mind be in you, making you humble and obedient to God's will:

And being found in fashion as a man, he humbled himself, and became obedient unto death, even the death of the cross. Wherefore God also hath highly exalted him, and given him a name which is above every name. That at the name of Jesus every knee should bow, of things in heaven, and things in earth, and things under the earth. And that every tongue should confess that Jesus Christ is Lord, to the glory of God the Father."

PHILIPPIANS 2:8–11, KJV

Know that all things were created by Jesus. He has authority over everything. It pleased God to make Jesus the Lord of all:

Jesus is the image of the invisible God, the firstborn of every creature. For by him were all things created, that are in heaven, and that are in earth, visible and invisible, whether they be thrones, or dominions, or principalities, or powers: all things were created by him, and for him. And he is before all things, and by him all things consist. And he is the head of the body, the church: who is the beginning, the firstborn from the dead; that in all things he might have the preeminence. For it pleased the Father that in him should all fulness dwell."

COLOSSIANS 1:15–19, KJV

Jesus Christ, the Word of God, is the beginning of all things:

> *In the beginning was the Word, and the Word was with God, and the Word was God. The same was in the beginning with God. All things were made by him; and without him was not anything made that was made. In him was life; and the life was the light of men. And the light shineth in darkness; and the darkness comprehended it not."*
>
> JOHN 1:1–5, KJV

> *And the Word was made flesh, and dwelt among us, (and we beheld his glory, the glory as of the only begotten of the Father,) full of grace and truth."*
>
> JOHN 1:14, KJV

Jesus Christ is the image of the unseen God, and it pleased the Father to give Him the supremacy over all things, seen or unseen.

THE NAME OF JESUS HEALS

Peter and John went into the temple at the hour of prayer. A man lame from his mother's womb was carried daily to the gate of the temple called Beautiful to ask for alms from the people. The lame man asked Peter and John for money, but Peter and John asked the lame man to look at them. The lame man looked at the disciples, expecting to receive something from them. Instead of obtaining money, he received something priceless. Peter and John called upon the mighty name of Jesus. The lame man received healing:

> *Then Peter said, Silver and gold have I none; but such as I have give I thee: In the name of Jesus Christ of Nazareth rise up and walk. And he took him by the right hand, and*

> *lifted him up: and immediately his feet and ankle bones received strength. And he leaping up stood, and walked, and entered with them into the temple, walking, and leaping, and praising God."*
>
> ACTS 3:6–8, KJV

I know my inheritance is in the Lord. I received supernatural healing, mentally and physically, by the power in the name and blood of Jesus. In May of 2009, I decided that I was going to fast, pray, praise, worship, and glorify the Lord at all times.

I worked the night shift as a registered nurse. At the end of an eight-hour shift one night, I felt a solid mass, or growth, in my mouth with my tongue. It was on my gum, at the lower right, near my wisdom teeth. When I got into my car, I pulled down the visor and looked into the mirror. It was hard, like a rock the size of a peanut, but it was not painful. I had decided that I was going to stay in the presence of the Lord, no matter what circumstance I faced. I believed it was a test from the enemy. I was not bothered at all by the growth.

Driving home from work, I had a conversation with the Lord. I had the impression, "Do not fast today." The direction given by the impression, I believe, was the Holy Spirit. I was to eat breakfast and go to bed. When I got home, I knelt to pray, praised, gave thanks, and worshiped. I ran my tongue around the growth and said healing Scriptures. I got up, ate breakfast, and went to bed. I slept for three hours. When I woke up, I checked the condition of the growth with my tongue. But there was no swelling. It had disappeared. I praised and worshiped. I know I did some new dancing steps to the glory of my God.

This particular event strengthened my Christian faith and my trust in God. The Word of God works, and divine healing is real. For those who know me, when you see me dance like David did, it is for the glory of God. I worship with all my heart, and I am not ashamed of the gospel of Christ. This healing experience is just one example of God's faithfulness to me.

HEALING PROMISES

I encourage you to locate the promises in the Word of God that relate to what you need for healing in your life, and then stand on it. Speak the Word to yourself and your circumstances, and it will increase your faith. According to Romans 10:17 (KJV), *"So then faith cometh by hearing, and hearing by the word of God."* I do this often and get positive results.

You must believe, reach out, and receive by faith. Hebrews 11:6 (KJV) states, *"But without faith it is impossible to please him: for he that cometh to God must believe that he is, and that he is a rewarder of them that diligently seek him."* You must participate in your healing process by praying, reaching out to the Lord by faith, and worshiping.

Even when it does not look like anything is happening, God is working behind the scenes. Look beyond the signs and symptoms, and trust God. The Word of God states that Jesus took the beating for you so that you can receive healing:

> *Surely he hath borne our griefs, and carried our sorrows: yet we did esteem him stricken, smitten of God, and afflicted. But he was wounded for our transgressions, he was bruised for our iniquities: the chastisement of our peace was upon him; and with his stripes we are healed. All we like sheep have gone astray; we have turned every one to his own way; and the Lord hath laid on him the iniquity of us all."*
>
> ISAIAH 53:4–6, KJV

CHOOSE HOW YOU WANT YOUR HEALING ANOINTING TO FLOW

With the knowledge that you were healed with His stripes, I encourage you to choose how you want your healing to manifest. Do you want it now, or would you rather debate and negotiate with the Lord? Remember that the Holy Spirit is gentle and flows in response to your faith.

For example, Jairus, a synagogue ruler, approached Jesus and asked Him to follow him to his house to heal his sick twelve-year-old daughter. On their way to Jairus's house, many people followed Jesus. One was a woman with an issue of blood. She did not negotiate with the Lord, but she acted in faith. She followed behind, touched Jesus's robe, and was healed instantly. Jesus perceived that virtue had gone out of Him, and He asked who had touched Him:

> *And Jesus said, Who touched me? When all denied, Peter and they that were with him said, Master, the multitude throng thee and press thee, and sayest thou, Who touched me? And Jesus said, Somebody hath touched me: for I perceive that virtue is gone out of me. And when the woman saw that she was not hid, she came trembling, and falling down before him, she declared unto him before all the people for what cause she had touched him, and how she was healed immediately."*
>
> LUKE 8:45–47, KJV

Jairus was okay with Jesus taking His time to follow him home. The woman with the issue of blood did not have that luxury. What if that was her last chance of ever coming in contact with the Savior? You decide how you want God's healing power to flow through you.

God honors His Word. Activate the power of God with the way you respond to His Word.

You may not need physical healing from the Lord. Whatever you are believing in God for now, know that He remains faithful to His Word. Abraham believed God and received Isaac in his old age. God was incredibly pleased with Abraham:

> *As it is written, I have made thee a father of many nations, before him whom he believed, even God, who quickeneth the dead, and calleth those things which be not as though they were. Who against hope believed in hope, that he might become the father of many nations, according to that which was spoken, So shall thy seed be. And being not weak in faith, he considered not his own body now dead, when he was about an hundred years old, neither yet the deadness of Sarah's womb: He staggered not at the promise of God through unbelief; but was strong in faith, giving glory to God; And being fully persuaded that, what he had promised, he was able also to perform. And therefore, it was imputed to him for righteousness."*
>
> ROMANS 4:17–22, KJV

God desires for you to know the riches of the glory of His inheritance:

> *That the God of our Lord Jesus Christ, the Father of glory, may give unto you the spirit of wisdom and revelation in the knowledge of him. The eyes of your understanding being enlightened; that ye may know what is the hope of his calling, and what the riches of the glory of his inheritance in the saints."*
>
> EPHESIANS 1:17–18, KJV

SUMMARY

In conclusion, when you know the importance of your position in Christ in the spirit realm, it gives you the confidence to trust Him and reach out to Him during challenging times. Knowing your position in Christ brings freedom and healing to your spirit, soul, and body.

PRAYER

Lord, thank You for the name of Jesus, the universal key that opens every door. I pray that You reveal to me my positional advantage in Christ. Lord, I thank You that I can come into Your presence with boldness and access Your throne room with confidence by the faith of the Lord Jesus Christ. Amen.

DECLARATION OF FAITH

Lord, I declare that I know my inheritance! I receive healing in my spirit, soul, and body because of my position in Christ.

ACTIVATION

- Ask God to reveal your position in Christ in the spirit realm.
- Ask the Lord to show you the riches of His inheritance's glory.
- Ask the Lord how your position in Christ brings you freedom.
- Ask God to reveal how your position in Christ heals your spirit, soul, and body.
- Write down what you hear.

SIX
PRAYING FOR THE WILL OF GOD

> *"And this is the confidence that we have in him, that, if we ask anything according to his will, he heareth us: And if we know that he hear us, whatsoever we ask, we know that we have the petitions that we desired of him."*
> —1 John 5:14–15, KJV—

When you pray according to God's will, it is comforting to know that difficult situations become more accessible as the grace of God takes over. If the enemy makes things difficult for you, know that the devil is no match for your God. Your life can be restored even in situations that look complicated or impossible.

Praying God's will can make things surprisingly bearable and manageable. Please know that no one is exempted from hardship. The Word confirms that there is a time for trouble. According to Ecclesiastes 3:1 (KJV), *"To everything there is a season, and a time to*

THE POWER OF COURAGEOUS FAITH

every purpose under the heaven." The Word tells us that there is *"A time to weep, and a time to laugh; a time to mourn, and a time to dance."*

You are not alone. If you are going through a turbulent time, pray for the will of God to take over.

PRAYING FOR THE WILL OF GOD IN DIFFICULT SITUATIONS

Even the Lord Jesus experienced difficult times. He went to Gethsemane to pray according to the will of God. Gethsemane was a terrible place for the Lord. All night, He prayed to receive grace to die for the redemption of men. Because Gethsemane is a sorrowful place to be, only take those that are close to the Lord when you feel it is time to go and pray:

> *Then cometh Jesus with them unto a place called Gethsemane, and saith unto the disciples, Sit ye here, while I go and pray yonder. And he took with him Peter and the two sons of Zebedee and began to be sorrowful and very heavy."*
>
> MATTHEW 26:36–37, KJV

In hell, Jesus, the King of kings and the Lord of lords, had to experience death and destruction to collect the keys from Satan. Jesus prayed the will of God, and our heavenly Father had mercy.

> *I am he that liveth, and was dead; and, behold, I am alive forevermore, Amen; and have the keys of hell and of death."*
>
> REVELATION 1:18, KJV

In addition to getting the keys, Jesus also received the gift of ministry for us.

> *But unto every one of us is given grace according to the measure of the gift of Christ. Wherefore he saith, when he ascended up on high, he led captivity captive, and gave gifts unto men."*
>
> EPHESIANS 4:7–8, KJV

Because He prayed according to the will of God, He had grace to go to the cross. You must spend time with the Lord and pray the will of God when you are at your Gethsemane. Your friends may fall asleep, but stay strong and trust God.

> *And he cometh unto the disciples, and findeth them asleep, and saith unto Peter, What, could ye not watch with me one hour? Watch and pray, that ye enter not into temptation: the spirit indeed is willing, but the flesh is weak."*
>
> MATTHEW 26:40–41, KJV

PRAYING GOD'S WILL GIVES HIM EASY ACCESS TO YOUR DIFFICULT CIRCUMSTANCES

The Lord commands you to be wise and understand the will of the Lord.[1] Do not pray amiss; for example, when you pray for God to give you a spouse, you cannot pray for God to provide you with a married man or a married woman. That is praying amiss.

> *Ye lust, and have not: ye kill, and desire to have, and cannot obtain: ye fight and war, yet ye have not, because ye ask not. Ye ask, and receive not, because ye ask amiss, that ye may consume it upon your lusts."*
>
> JAMES 4:2–3, KJV

Allowing the Lord to have His way in your life is imperative. As a result, the Lord encourages you to pray according to His will: *"After this manner therefore pray ye: Our Father which art in heaven, Hallowed be thy name. Thy kingdom come, thy will be done in earth, as it is in heaven"* (Matthew 6:9–10, KJV).

GOD FOUGHT FOR ISRAEL WHEN THEY PRAYED THE WILL OF GOD

When the king of Egypt became aware that the Israelites had fled, the hearts of Pharaoh and his servants turned against the Israelites, and they said, *"Why have we done this, that we have let Israel go from serving us?"* (Exodus 14:5, KJV). Pharaoh's chariots and his host were no match for the God of Israel. Because the Israelites prayed, it was God's will for the children of Israel to leave Egypt. The people of Israel called on the Lord to deliver them from the Egyptian armies, and God fought for them:

> *And the waters returned, and covered the chariots, and the horsemen, and all the host of Pharaoh that came into the sea after them; there remained not so much as one of them. But the children of Israel walked upon dry land in the midst of the sea; and the waters were a wall unto them on their right hand, and on their left. Thus, the Lord saved Israel that day out of the hand of the Egyptians; and Israel saw the Egyptians dead upon the seashore. And Israel saw that great work which the Lord did upon the Egyptians: and the people feared the Lord, and believed the Lord, and his servant Moses."*
>
> EXODUS 14:28–31, KJV

GOLIATH DEFYING THE ARMIES OF ISRAEL PROVOKED GOD

The Philistines provoked the Lord when they defied the armies of Israel. The Israelites cried out to God. God had mercy and sent David to deliver Israel from Goliath:

> *And he stood and cried unto the armies of Israel, and said unto them, Why are ye come out to set your battle in array? am not I a Philistine, and ye servants to Saul? choose you a man for you, and let him come down to me. If he be able to fight with me, and to kill me, then will we be your servants: but if I prevail against him, and kill him, then shall ye be our servants, and serve us. And the Philistine said, I defy the armies of Israel this day; give me a man, that we may fight together."*
>
> 1 SAMUEL 17:8–10, KJV

David related to Saul how he had fought with a lion and a bear. He persuaded King Saul to give him permission to go and fight Goliath:

> *The Lord that delivered me out of the paw of the lion, and out of the paw of the bear, he will deliver me out of the hand of this Philistine. And Saul said unto David, Go, and the Lord be with thee."*
>
> 1 SAMUEL 17:37, KJV

It was the will of God for the children of Israel to be delivered from the Philistines. David prayed according to the will of God, and God favored him:

THE POWER OF COURAGEOUS FAITH   75

> *Then said David to the Philistine, Thou comest to me with a sword, and with a spear, and with a shield: but I come to thee in the name of the Lord of hosts, the God of the armies of Israel, whom thou hast defied. This day will the Lord deliver thee into mine hand; and I will smite thee, and take thine head from thee; and I will give the carcases of the host of the Philistines this day unto the fowls of the air, and to the wild beasts of the earth; that all the earth may know that there is a God in Israel."*
>
> 1 SAMUEL 17:45–46, KJV

When Goliath approached David to attack him, David was overshadowed by the spirit of boldness from God. He ran toward the army to meet the Philistine:

> *And it came to pass, when the Philistine arose, and came, and drew nigh to meet David, that David hastened, and ran toward the army to meet the Philistine. And David put his hand in his bag, and took thence a stone, and slang it, and smote the Philistine in his forehead, that the stone sunk into his forehead; and he fell upon his face to the earth. So, David prevailed over the Philistine with a sling and with a stone, and smote the Philistine, and slew him; but there was no sword in the hand of David. Therefore, David ran, and stood upon the Philistine, and took his sword, and drew it out of the sheath thereof, and slew him, and cut off his head therewith. And when the Philistines saw their champion was dead, they fled."*
>
> 1 SAMUEL 17:48–51, KJV

When you pray according to God's will, you will return from your battlefront spiritually or physically with the head of your enemy in your hand, just like David did: *"And as David returned from the slaughter of the Philistine, Abner took him, and brought him before Saul with the head of the Philistine in his hand"* (1 Samuel 17:57, KJV).

PRAYING GOD'S WILL REVEALS HIS PURPOSE FOR YOU

When we pray according to His will, God reveals His will to us. Ephesians 1:11 (KJV) communicates that *"we have obtained an inheritance, being predestined according to the purpose of him who worketh all things after the counsel of his own will."* As you pray and wait on the Lord, it is comforting to know that He desires to reveal to you His will for your life:

> *Having made known unto us the mystery of his will, according to his good pleasure which he hath purposed in himself: That in the dispensation of the fulness of times he might gather together in one all things in Christ, both which are in heaven, and which are on earth; even in him."*
>
> EPHESIANS 1:9–10, KJV

Continue to make a conscientious effort toward seeking and knowing God. He will reward you with answers.

PRAYING THE WILL OF GOD BEFORE MAKING SIGNIFICANT DECISIONS

The Lord Jesus did not take selecting His twelve disciples lightly. He was intentional, and He knew it was crucial to pray according to the will of God with wisdom all night before choosing His disciples: *"And it came to pass in those days, that he went out into a mountain to pray, and continued all night in prayer to God. And when it was day, he called unto him his disciples: and of them he chose twelve, whom also he named apostles" (Luke 6:12–13, KJV).

Before making any major decision, you must also pray according to the will of God for wisdom and direction. Jesus prayed, *"Not as I will, but as thou wilt."* By doing this, He received grace to go to the cross: "Then saith he unto them, My soul is exceeding sorrowful, even unto death: tarry ye here, and watch with me. And he went a little farther, and fell on his face, and prayed, saying, O my Father, if it be possible, let this cup pass from me: nevertheless not as I will, but as thou wilt" (Matthew 26:38–39, KJV).

THE ABSENCE OF PEACE AND JOY

In order to adequately discern the things of the spirit, the Word of God needs to dwell in you. The Word of God is a guide. When you pray for the will of God, the Lord will confirm it with peace as a sign that you can proceed.

When you pray, check for the presence of peace and joy. The peace and joy of God accompanies His agreement if you are praying according to the will of God.

> *For the kingdom of God is not meat and drink; but righteousness, and peace, and joy in the Holy Ghost. For he that in these things serveth Christ is acceptable to God, and approved of men. Let us therefore follow after the things which make for peace, and things wherewith one may edify another."*
>
> ROMANS 14:17–19, KJV

Psalm 23 explains what happens when you pray the will of God: *"He maketh me to lie down in green pastures: he leadeth me beside the still waters. He restoreth my soul: he leadeth me in the paths of righteousness for his name's sake. Yea, though I walk through the valley of the shadow of death, I will fear no evil: for thou art with me; thy rod and thy staff they comfort me"* (Psalm 23:2–4, KJV).

PRAYING THE WILL OF GOD BRINGS HEAVENLY VISITATIONS AND DREAMS

The Lord promised to pour His Spirit out upon everyone in the last days. When you pray according to the will of God and know His Word, He may visit you in your dreams with vital information:

> *And it shall come to pass in the last days, saith God, I will pour out of my Spirit upon all flesh: and your sons and your daughters shall prophesy, and your young men shall see visions, and your old men shall dream dreams."*
>
> ACTS 2:17, KJV

The Lord can reveal important information when you pray according to the will of God. Joseph prayed according to the will of God, and God revealed His will to Joseph in a dream. It was the will of God for Mary to conceive and give birth to Jesus, although she was a virgin. Her husband, Joseph, intended to let her go because they were never intimate, but he was warned in a dream not to separate from her:

> *Then Joseph her husband, being a just man, and not willing to make her a public example, was minded to put her away privily. But while he thought on these things, behold, the angel of the Lord appeared unto him in a dream, saying, Joseph, thou son of David, fear not to take unto thee Mary thy wife: for that which is conceived in her is of the Holy Ghost."*
>
> MATTHEW 1:19–20, KJV

When Jesus was born, wise men came from the east to Jerusalem, asking about Jesus. They saw His star in the east and came to worship Him. When Herod, the king, heard these things, he was troubled. He gathered all the chief priests and scribes. He asked where Christ would be born and was told in Bethlehem of Judaea.

Herod called the wise men and asked them what time the star would appear and sent them to Bethlehem to search for Jesus, asking them to inform him when they found Jesus so he could worship Him also. But the wise men were warned in a dream by God that they should not return to Herod: *"And being warned of God in a dream that they should not return to Herod, they departed into their own country another way"* (Matthew 2:12, KJV).

An angel of the Lord instructed Joseph in a dream to take Jesus to Egypt. Herod was angry and ordered the murder of all male children two years old or under: *"Then Herod, when he saw that he was mocked of the wise men, was exceeding wroth, and sent forth, and slew all the children that were in Bethlehem, and in all the coasts thereof, from two years old and under, according to the time which he had diligently inquired of the wise men"* (Matthew 2:13–16, KJV).

SUMMARY

You are not alone. When you pray according to God's will, you receive grace to overcome challenges.

If you are going through a turbulent time, pray with confidence: *"And this is the confidence that we have in him, that, if we ask anything according to his will, he heareth us: And if we know that he hear us, whatsoever we ask, we know that we have the petitions that we desired of him"* (1 John 5:14–15, KJV).

PRAYER

Father, thank You for teaching me to pray according to Your will. Lord, I pray that You give me the confidence to present my petition to You according to Your will. Help me to be willing and obedient to Your calling. Lord, I pray that You give me the grace to pray for and accept Your will for my life. Amen.

DECLARATION OF FAITH

Lord, I declare that Your will is done in my life. I receive the grace to accept Your perfect will for my life.

ACTIVATION

- Ask God to reveal His perfect will for your life.
- Ask the Lord to give you the grace to accept His will for your life.
- Ask the Lord what you need to surrender to Him.
- Write down what you hear.

SEVEN
WEAPONS OF WARFARE: PRAISE, THANKSGIVING, AND WORSHIP

> *"O praise the Lord, all ye nations:*
> *praise him, all ye people. For his merciful*
> *kindness is great toward us:*
> *and the truth of the Lord endureth forever.*
> *Praise ye the Lord."*
> **—Psalm 117:1–2, KJV—**

Praise, thanksgiving, and worship are instruments and weapons of spiritual warfare. For effective warfare, you need spiritual, physical, and psychological processes, such as cognition, perception, attention, and emotion. You need to be ready and fully present to fight and win. You must practice using your instruments often and prepare for warfare in advance. When you prepare for the battle, you maximize your chances of winning.

Be warned. Do not wait for the enemy to be at your doorstep before you learn how to use your weapons. The enemy does not play games.

He is very subtle; while it may seem like he is joking with you, he is not. Please be intentional. You will have to use these weapons sooner or later. Because of this, you need wisdom, knowledge, and understanding of the Word of God to use them skillfully. In this chapter we will discuss how, when, and why you should use these instruments of war.

PREPARING FOR BATTLE

Times of peace and rest are the perfect times to use these instruments of warfare. Take the spirit of joy and laugh, dance, and have fun with the Lord.

In times of turbulence, trouble, destitution, failure, obstacles, and more, invite the Lord Jesus into your life. Allow the Holy Spirit to take total control. Then ask the Lord to give you the grace to use your instruments well. Remember, faith comes by hearing the Word of God. Pray it out loud, praise, give thanks in advance for your victory, and then invoke the presence of the Almighty God by worshiping.

Crying or weeping before the Lord is another effective tool to fight the enemy. When I use these instruments of war, the Lord shows up and brings with Him supernatural peace. At this point, the Lord brings joy and laughter, even amid fire: *"He that sitteth in the heavens shall laugh: the Lord shall have them in derision"* (Psalm 2:4, KJV).

MULTIPLICATION HAPPENS WHEN YOU PRAISE THE LORD

Remember my prayer partner (Maggie) who was barren for eighteen years? To give glory to the Lord for her beautiful daughter and His faithfulness to Maggie, we praised, gave thanks, and worshiped. What happened next will encourage you to begin to use these instruments in your spiritual battles!

As we danced before the Lord, as David did, our blessings multiplied. Praise provoked God positively. The Lord responded to His Word and decided to bless Maggie with two handsome boys in addition to the first girl. Hallelujah!

The Lord revealed the secret to multiplication. It is in the Word: pray, praise, give thanks, and worship. I encourage you to praise and worship God as often as possible. These are spiritual keys that open impossible doors. When you begin to praise and worship the Lord, ancient doors are forced open for the King of glory to enter.

> *Lift up your heads, O ye gates; and be ye lift up, ye everlasting doors; and the King of glory shall come in. Who is this King of glory? The Lord strong and mighty, the Lord mighty in battle. Lift up your heads, O ye gates; even lift them up, ye everlasting doors; and the King of glory shall come in."*
>
> PSALM 24:7–9, KJV

When Jesus prayed and gave thanks, multiplication happened. At the sea of Tiberias, a great multitude followed Him. Jesus could see the hunger in their eyes. He had compassion for the people and fed them both spiritually and physically.

Jesus asked Philip where they could buy bread to feed the multitude. Andrew replied that a man had five barley loaves and two small fishes, but what were they among so many? Jesus said, "Make the men sit down." Five thousand men sat down to eat. Jesus gave thanks, and five barley loaves and two small fishes multiplied to feed the people:

> *And Jesus took the loaves; and when he had given thanks, he distributed to the disciples, and the disciples to them that were set down; and likewise of the fishes as much as*

they would. When they were filled, he said unto his disciples, Gather up the fragments that remain, that nothing be lost. Therefore they gathered them together, and filled twelve baskets with the fragments of the five barley loaves, which remained over and above unto them that had eaten."

JOHN 6:11–13, KJV

God is not a respecter of persons. If God did it for Jesus and Maggie, He can do it for you, too. Try using the weapons of your warfare as often as possible for multiplied blessings. These weapons are lethal to the kingdom of darkness.

THE POWER OF THESE WEAPONS AT MIDNIGHT

Psalm 91:5–6 (KJV) says, *"Thou shalt not be afraid for the terror by night; nor for the arrow that flieth by day; Nor for the pestilence that walketh in darkness; nor for the destruction that wasteth at noonday."* Praise, thanksgiving, and worship as instruments or weapons of spiritual warfare are effective. When I use them at midnight, demons flee and the peace of God takes over. Empirical evidence shows that these weapons triumph over evil. When Paul and Silas were in prison, they used these instruments of war:

And at midnight Paul and Silas prayed and sang praises unto God: and the prisoners heard them."

ACTS 16:25, KJV

Because Paul and Silas used these weapons, the prison could not contain them. The prison had to eject them. The Lord showed up for them, and His presence was great. What happened to them was amazing. Their chains came off, and they were delivered and released supernaturally from prison:

> *And suddenly there was a great earthquake, so that the foundations of the prison were shaken: and immediately all the doors were opened, and everyone's bands were loosed."*
>
> ACTS 16:26, KJV

PRAISE MOVES THE LORD TO FIGHT AGAINST YOUR ENEMIES

A great multitude came against Jehoshaphat to battle. Afraid, he set himself to seek the Lord and proclaimed a fast throughout all Judah:

> *And when he had consulted with the people, he appointed singers unto the Lord, and that should praise the beauty of holiness, as they went out before the army, and to say, Praise the Lord; for his mercy endureth forever. And when they began to sing and to praise, the Lord set ambushments against the children of Ammon, Moab, and mount Seir, which were come against Judah; and they were smitten. For the children of Ammon and Moab stood up against the inhabitants of mount Seir, utterly to slay and destroy them: and when they had made an end of the inhabitants of Seir, everyone helped to destroy another. And when Judah came toward the watch tower in the wilderness, they looked unto the multitude, and behold, they were dead bodies fallen to the earth, and none escaped."*
>
> 2 CHRONICLES 20:21–24, KJV

King Sennacherib sent a letter to King Hezekiah that mocked the God of Israel and threatened to come and take the people of Israel away.

Hezekiah took the letter to the temple of the Lord and presented it to God, saying:

> *O Lord of hosts, God of Israel, that dwellest between the cherubim, thou art the God, even thou alone, of all the kingdoms of the earth: thou hast made heaven and earth. Incline thine ear, O Lord, and hear; open thine eyes, O Lord, and see and hear all the words of Sennacherib, which hath sent to reproach the living God."*
>
> ISAIAH 37:16–17, KJV

Hezekiah acknowledged that the kings of Assyria had destroyed all other nations and cast their man-made gods into the fire, which is why the kings of Assyria could overtake them. Hezekiah persuaded the Lord, saying, *"O Lord our God, save us from his hand, that all the kingdoms of the earth may know that thou art the Lord, even thou only"* (Isaiah 37:20, KJV). The people of Israel felt insulted by Sennacherib for disrespecting the God of Israel. Rabshakeh delivered these messages from the king of Assyria and proceeded to blaspheme the name of the God of Israel, saying:

> *Beware lest Hezekiah persuade you, saying, the Lord will deliver us. Hath any of the gods of the nations delivered his land out of the hand of the king of Assyria? Where are the gods of Hamath and Arphad? where are the gods of Sepharvaim? and have they delivered Samaria out of my hand? Who are they among all the gods of these lands, that have delivered their land out of my hand, that the Lord should deliver Jerusalem out of my hand?"*
>
> ISAIAH 36:18–20, KJV

King Hezekiah received the message, rented his clothes, covered himself with sackcloth, and went into the house of the Lord. King Hezekiah sent Eliakim and Shebna, the scribe, and the elders of the priests covered with sackcloth to Isaiah the prophet. The messengers delivered the message, and King Hezekiah lamented, *"This day is a day of trouble, rebuke, and blasphemy"* (Isaiah 37:3, KJV). Isaiah asked Eliakim, Shebna, and the elders of the priests to tell King Hezekiah that God said he should not be afraid of the words of the king of Assyria. The Lord said He would send a blast upon him. He also said Sennacherib would hear a rumor, return to his land, and fall by the sword in his land.

> *Then the angel of the Lord went forth and smote in the camp of the Assyrians a hundred and fourscore and five thousand: and when they arose early in the morning, behold, they were all dead corpses. So, Sennacherib king of Assyria departed, and went and returned, and dwelt at Nineveh. And it came to pass, as he was worshiping in the house of Nisroch his god, that Adrammelech and Sharezer his sons smote him with the sword; and they escaped into the land of Armenia: and Esarhaddon his son reigned in his stead."*
>
> ISAIAH 37:36–38, KJV

Sennacherib, the king of Assyria, blasphemed the name of the Lord. Hezekiah presented his exhortation to the Lord, which provoked Him. Because of Hezekiah's reminder that God is the only God in all the earth, He miraculously delivered the children of Israel from Sennacherib. The Bible encourages us that everything that can breathe should praise God:

> *Praise ye the Lord. Praise God in his sanctuary: praise him in the firmament of his power. Praise him for his mighty*

acts: praise him according to his excellent greatness. Praise him with the sound of the trumpet: praise him with the psaltery and harp. Praise him with the timbrel and dance: praise him with stringed instruments and organs. Praise him upon the loud cymbals: praise him upon the high-sounding cymbals. Let everything that hath breath praise the Lord. Praise ye the Lord."

PSALM 150:1–6, KJV

THANKSGIVING

O give thanks unto the Lord; for he is good: because his mercy endureth forever."

PSALM 118:1, KJV

The Bible asserts we should approach the Lord with thanksgiving: *"Enter into his gates with thanksgiving, and into his courts with praise: be thankful unto him and bless his name"* (Psalm 100:4, KJV). And Paul wrote, *"And whatsoever ye do in word or deed, do all in the name of the Lord Jesus, giving thanks to God and the Father by him"* (Colossians 3:17, KJV).

The children of Israel took giving thanks to the Lord seriously and appointed six men to ensure that giving of thanks to the Lord was executed properly: *"Moreover, the Levites: Jeshua, Binnui, Kadmiel, Sherebiah, Judah, and Mattaniah, which was over the thanksgiving, he and his brethren"* (Nehemiah 12:8, KJV).

The Bible commands that you should be generous with giving thanks to your creator: *"O give thanks unto the Lord; for he is good: for his mercy endureth forever. O give thanks unto the God of gods: for his* mercy endureth forever. O give thanks to the Lord of Lords: for his mercy endureth forever" (Psalm 136:1–3, KJV).

Be reminded that giving thanks is good: *"It is a good thing to give thanks unto the Lord, and to sing praises unto thy name, O Most High"* (Psalm 92:1, KJV).

WORSHIP INVOKES THE PRESENCE OF GOD

O worship the Lord in the beauty of holiness: fear before him, all the earth."

PSALM 96:1, KJV

Solomon praised, gave thanks, and worshiped. Solomon blessed the Lord God of Israel, who fulfilled what Solomon spoke to his father, David. Solomon lifted the name of the Lord, telling Him *"there is no God like thee in the heaven, nor in the earth, which keeps covenant, and showiest mercy unto His servants, that walk before Him with all their hearts"* (2 Chronicles 6:14, KJV).

Solomon was generous with adoration, exaltation, and lifting the name of the Lord:

Now, my God, let, I beseech thee, thine eyes be open, and let thine ears be attend unto the prayer that is made in this place. Now therefore arise, O Lord God, into thy resting place, thou, and the ark of thy strength: let thy priests, O Lord God, be clothed with salvation, and let thy saints rejoice in goodness. O Lord God, turn not away the face of thine anointed: remember the mercies of David thy servant."

2 CHRONICLES 6:40–42, KJV

Solomon impressed the Lord with his glorification. As a result of King Solomon's reverence of the Lord, showing the people that the Lord is high and lifted, Solomon invoked the presence of God, who showed up and received the sacrifice that King Solomon and the people presented. In addition, the people worshiped the Lord willingly.

> *Now when Solomon had made an end of praying, the fire came down from heaven, and consumed the burnt offering and the sacrifices; and the glory of the Lord filled the house. And the priests could not enter into the house of the Lord, because the glory of the Lord had filled the Lord's house. And when all the children of Israel saw how the fire came down, and the glory of the Lord upon the house, they bowed themselves with their faces to the ground upon the pavement, and worshiped, and praised the Lord, saying, for he is good; for his mercy endureth forever."*
>
> 2 CHRONICLES 7:1–3, KJV

SUMMARY

In summary, praise, thanksgiving, and worship are instruments or weapons of spiritual warfare. Using your weapons frequently and consistently is essential because the enemy is not backing down. Be ready to engage in this warfare at any time, and take the spirit of joy with you. When you do this, you confuse the enemy and release the presence of God.

PRAYER

My soul blesses You, Lord. Thank You for all Your goodness in my life. Thank You for salvation, blessing me with Your healing power and giving me divine health. Thank You for Your tender mercies and Your loving kindness. Thank You for visiting me and for crowning my years with Your goodness. Lord, I do not take Your love for me for granted. I appreciate that You satisfy my mouth with good things and renew my youth like the eagle's.

DECLARATION OF FAITH

Lord, I magnify and exalt Your name. I will bless You at all times, and Your praise shall continually be in my mouth.

ACTIVATION

- Ask God to show you how to utilize praise, thanksgiving, and worship as weapons of warfare.
- Ask the Lord to show you how not to worry, but in everything by prayer and supplication with thanksgiving, make your request known to Him.
- Ask the Lord to show you how using your weapons of war moves Him to fight your battles.
- Ask God to give you the grace to bless Him at all times.
- Write down what you hear.

EIGHT
WHEN YOU MAKE A VOW TO THE LORD, FOLLOW THROUGH

> *"When thou shalt vow a vow unto the Lord thy God, thou shalt not slack to pay it: for the Lord thy God will surely require it of thee; and it would be sin in thee. But if thou shalt forbear to vow, it shall be no sin in thee. That which is gone out of thy lips thou shalt keep and perform; even a freewill offering, according as thou hast vowed unto the Lord thy God, which thou hast promised with thy mouth."*
> —**Deuteronomy 23:21–23, KJV**—

A vow is a promise you make to the Lord. In some ways and in some circumstances, a vow can be a way of bargaining with the Lord. For example, if you need a favor from God, you might tell the Lord you will give whatever you promised if He fulfills your specific petition. Usually, when someone is in a desperate position, nothing seems to be working out, and all doors seem closed, people tend to do or say whatever it takes to get out of the situation. As a child of God, you should ensure that your words and actions align with the Word of God.

Don't take it lightly or irreverently when you make vows to the Lord in prayer. Honor the Lord in every situation you find yourself in, and uphold your promises to Him.

THE RULES OF MAKING A VOW

Before you make a vow, familiarize yourself with what the Word says. You are not obligated to make vows. For any that you make, the Lord will hold you accountable. May the Lord help you keep your promises to Him when you make them.

> *If a man vows a vow unto the Lord or swear an oath to bind his soul with a bond; he shall not break his word, he shall do according to all that proceedeth out of his mouth."*
>
> NUMBERS 30:2, KJV

1. **The Lord holds His words in high regards:**

"My covenant will I not break, nor alter the thing that is gone out of my lips."—Psalm 89:34, KJV

2. **God expects that you keep your words:**

"That which is gone out of thy lips thou shalt keep and perform; even a freewill offering, according as thou hast vowed unto the Lord thy God, which thou hast promised with thy mouth."—Deuteronomy 23:23, KJV

3. **Because it is easy to forget if you make an oath to God, the Lord encourages you not to make them:**

"Again, ye have heard that it hath been said by them of old time, thou shalt not forswear thyself, but shalt perform unto the Lord thine oaths."
—Matthew 5:33, KJV

4. The principles in the Bible are there to remind you to follow the Word as written. The Lord takes His words seriously, and so should you:

"Forever, O Lord, thy word is settled in heaven." —Psalm 119:89, KJV

5. The Lord states that you will explain every word you speak:

"But I say unto you, that every idle word that men shall speak, they shall give account thereof in the day of judgment." —Matthew 12:36, KJV

When you say things to God in your prayer time with Him, it is vital that you keep the words you uttered, especially if you intentionally tell Him, "God, if you get me out of this mess, I will do so and so." The Lord sees this as making a covenant with Him.

6. The Lord said He does not break His covenants:

"My covenant will I not break nor alter the thing that is gone out of my lips." —Psalm 89:34, KJV

For example, getting married involves you making a vow to God that you intend to keep that marriage. Make sure you hear from God. Do not allow anyone to push you into marriage without counting the cost; do in-depth research about what God says about marriage. Be very sure you hear from God before you commit.

GOD HONORED MY VOW

In high school, my dream profession was to become a nurse. In my mind, this could only be possible if God intervened. I approached my dad and explained to him what was on my mind, and I asked him to take me to the church to pray. He agreed and took me.

When we got to the church, the attendant was present. My dad explained the reason why we were there. The older man and my dad prayed for me, and I made the vow: if God made it possible for me to gain admission into the best nursing school in Nigeria and become a trained nurse, I would return and pay my vow. My dad agreed with me, blessed me, and wrote down and dated the vow. God answered that prayer, and I am careful to return all the glory to Him.

I gained admission into the School of Nursing at the Lagos University Teaching Hospital, completed my studies, and became a registered nurse and midwife. When I returned to the church years later, I was grateful to the Lord for keeping my dad and the church attendant alive. They were able to pray and thank the Lord with me for completing my degree as a trained nurse.

Every time I think of this, it brings tears to my eyes. God is faithful, and He keeps His word. To experience the faithfulness of God as a teenager solidified my trust in Him. The making and paying of vows is scriptural. Present your supplication to the Lord. If you feel led to make a vow, make it and write it down. Do not sin against God by forgetting to pay for the vow that you made.

> *Better is it that thou shouldest not vow, than that thou shouldest vow and not pay."*
>
> ECCLESIASTES 5:5, KJV

HANNAH MADE AND PAID HER VOW TO THE LORD

God's Word must dwell richly in you so that you will be mindful of what comes out of your mouth, especially when you make vows.

As mentioned in chapter 3, Hannah sought the Lord because she knew the Word of God and believed He answered prayer. When Peninnah, her adversary, mocked her about not being able to have children, Hannah sought the Lord. She wept before Him and made a vow. This chapter explores Hannah's pain, the vow she made, and the result.

 And she vowed a vow, and said, O Lord of hosts, if thou wilt indeed look on the affliction of thine handmaid, and remember me, and not forget thine handmaid, but wilt give unto thine handmaid a man child, then I will give him unto the Lord all the days of his life, and there shall no razor come upon his head."

1 SAMUEL 1:11, KJV

Desperate, Hannah went to the temple to present her case before the Lord. Eli, a priest and a prophet, watched as Hannah pleaded with the Lord, interceding for herself. Only her lips moved. Eli thought Hannah was drunk and said, *"How long wilt thou be drunken? put away thy wine from thee. And Hannah answered and said, No, my Lord, I am a woman of a sorrowful spirit: I have drunk neither wine nor strong drink, but have poured out my soul before the Lord"* (1 Samuel 1:13–14, KJV).

When Eli heard why Hannah was seeking God, he blessed Hannah and sent her away in peace, saying, *"The God of Israel grant thee thy petition that thou hast asked of him. And she said, let thine handmaid find grace in thy sight. So, the woman went her way, and did eat, and her countenance was no more sad"* (1 Samuel 1:17–18, KJV).

Hannah knew the power of the Word of God. She believed Eli when he asked God to grant her petition. Hannah believed in the Word of God, and she was established. She believed the prophet Eli, and she prospered: *"Believe in the Lord your God so shall ye be established; believe his prophets, so shall ye prosper"* (2 Chronicles 20:20, KJV).

Hannah conceived, delivered a son, and named him Samuel. Hannah took care of her son, and after she weaned him, she brought him to the prophet Eli as she had promised the Lord. She paid her vow:

> *And they slew a bullock and brought the child to Eli. And she said, Oh my Lord, as thy soul liveth, my Lord, I am the woman that stood by thee here, praying unto the Lord. For this child I prayed; and the Lord hath given me my petition which I asked of him: Therefore, also I have lent him to the Lord; as long as he liveth he shall be lent to the Lord. And he worshiped the Lord there."*
>
> 1 SAMUEL 1:17–18, KJV

God answered Hannah's prayer and blessed her with Samuel, one of God's greatest prophets. In addition, God surprised Hannah with more children for her obedience: *"And the Lord visited Hannah, so that she conceived, and bare three sons and two daughters. And the child Samuel grew before the Lord"* (1 Samuel 2:21, KJV).

This story beautifully illustrates the power of making and keeping a vow.

DAVID AND JONATHAN

Because King Saul had determined to kill David, David was afraid for his life. He fled, and when he found Jonathan, he said, *"What have I done? What is mine iniquity? and what is my sin before thy father, that he seeketh my life?"* (1 Samuel 20:1, KJV).

Jonathan had compassion for David because he loved him. Jonathan promised David that he would make him aware if his life was in danger and to send him away if he was:

 The Lord do so and much more to Jonathan: but if it please my father to do thee evil, then I will shew it thee, and send thee away, that thou mayest go in peace: and the Lord be with thee, as he hath been with my father. And thou shalt not only while yet I live shew me the kindness of the Lord, that I die not. But also thou shalt not cut off thy kindness from my house for ever: no, not when the Lord hath cut off the enemies of David everyone from the face of the earth."

1 SAMUEL 20:13–15, KJV

Then David and Jonathan made a vow: *"And Jonathan said to David, Go in peace, forasmuch as we have sworn both of us in the name of the Lord, saying, The Lord be between me and thee, and between my seed and thy seed forever. And he arose and departed: and Jonathan went into the city"* (1 Samuel 20:42, KJV).

David, the man after God's heart, knew the power of the Word of God. After he became king, he made good on his vow to Jonathan: *"And David said, is there yet any that is left of the house of Saul, that I may shew him kindness for Jonathan's sake?"* (2 Samuel 9:1, KJV).

David summoned Ziba, a servant of the house of Saul, who confirmed that Jonathan had a son. David sent for him: *"Then king David sent, and fetched him out of the house of Machir, the son of Ammiel, from Lodebar. Now when Mephibosheth, the son of Jonathan, the son of Saul, was come unto David, he fell on his face, and did reverence. And David said, Mephibosheth. And he answered, Behold thy servant"* (2 Samuel 9:5–6, KJV).

THE POWER OF COURAGEOUS FAITH 99

Mephibosheth, the son of Jonathan, appeared before King David. David honored God by keeping the vow that he made to Jonathan while Jonathan was alive:

> *And David said unto him, Fear not: for I will surely shew thee kindness for Jonathan thy father's sake and will restore thee all the land of Saul thy father; and thou shalt eat bread at my table continually. And Mephibosheth had a young son, whose name was Micha. And all that dwelt in the house of Ziba were servants unto Mephibosheth. So Mephibosheth dwelt in Jerusalem: for he did eat continually at the king's table; and was lame on both his feet."*
>
> 2 SAMUEL 9:5–6, KJV

EVIL VOWS

Not every vow made brings glory to God. Before you make a vow, it is essential to know the power of God's Word with wisdom and be aware of the words you speak. For example, Jephthah used his words to bring misery to himself:

> *And Jephthah vowed a vow unto the Lord, and said, if thou shalt without fail deliver the children of Ammon into mine hands. Then it shall be, that whatsoever cometh forth of the doors of my house to meet me, when I return in peace from the children of Ammon, shall surely be the Lord's, and I will offer it up for a burnt offering. So, Jephthah passed over unto the children of Ammon to fight against them; and the Lord delivered them into his hands. And he smote them from Aroer, even till thou come to Minnith, even twenty cities, and unto the plain of the vineyards, with a very great slaughter. Thus, the children of Ammon were subdued before the children of Israel. And Jephthah came to Mizpah*

> *unto his house, and behold, his daughter came out to meet him with timbrels and with dances: and she was his only child; beside her he had neither son nor daughter."*

JUDGES 11:30–34, KJV

Note that Jephthah was not obligated to make such a vow to the Lord, and the Lord did not make Jephthah's daughter go out to meet him. Be careful with your words. They can be a blessing or a curse.

We see another example of this in a New Testament story from the life of Paul. Over forty Jewish men banded together and bound themselves under a curse, saying they would neither eat nor drink until they killed Paul. They presented their case to the chief priests and elders: *"Now therefore ye with the council signify to the chief captain that he bring him down unto you tomorrow, as though ye would enquire something more perfectly concerning him: and we, or ever he come near, are ready to kill him"* (Acts 23:15, KJV).

Paul's nephew heard of their lying-in-wait and entered the castle. He revealed the plot to Paul, who asked him to relate the message to the chief captain:

> *So, the chief captain then let the young man depart, and charged him, See thou tell no man that thou hast shewed these things to me. And he called unto him two centurions, saying, make ready two hundred soldiers to go to Caesarea, and horsemen threescore and ten, and spearmen two hundred, at the third hour of the night. And provide them beasts, that they may set Paul on, and bring him safe unto Felix the governor."*

ACTS 23:22–23, KJV

The chief priests, elders, and chief captain understood the significance and the urgency of getting Paul to safety because they understood the power of oaths and vows. Paul's nephew saved his life.

SUMMARY

Vows have a place in our relationship and prayer life with the Lord. However, they must be taken very seriously. If God kept His part of the deal, you should also keep your part of the deal. When you do, you allow the Spirit of God to direct and have access to your life. It brings you closer to the Lord, and according to the Word, there is rest for your soul: *"The Lord preserveth the simple: I was brought low, and he helped me. Return unto thy rest, O my soul; for the Lord hath dealt bountifully with thee"* (Psalm 116:6–7, KJV).

Please pay your vow. Remember that you have a merciful God.

PRAYER POINT

Dear God, thank You for preserving my life because of Your loving kindness. Lord, while I continue seeking Your face, please help me write down and fulfill my promises when in Your presence. And thank You, Lord, for keeping Your promises to me. Amen.

DECLARATION OF FAITH

The Lord keeps His promises for me. I choose to keep my promises to Him as well.

ACTIVATION

- Ask the Lord to show you any forgotten promises and repent.

- Ask the Lord to show you one thing that you need to do today for the Lord to open your windows of Heaven and pour down blessings into your life.
- Ask the Lord to help you take His Word seriously and keep your promises.
- Write down what you hear.

NINE
FINDING PEACE IN ANY SITUATION

"And the peace of God, which passeth all understanding, shall keep your hearts and minds through Christ Jesus. Finally, brethren, whatsoever things are true, whatsoever things are honest, whatsoever things are just, whatsoever things are pure, whatsoever things are lovely, whatsoever things are of good report; if there be any virtue, and if there be any praise, think on these things. Those things, which ye have both learned, and received, and heard, and seen in me, do: and the God of peace shall be with you."
—**Philippians 4:7–9, KJV**—

Peace is the freedom from agitation or disturbance from fear, terror, anger, or anxiety; quietness of mind; tranquility; calmness; and quiet of conscience.[1] Peace is priceless. When you find it, the enemy will try as hard as he can to steal it. He can emplcy anyone who makes themselves available to accomplish it.

Remember, not everyone wants to live peaceably. Some people thrive only where there is discord, trouble, and confusion. When you try to make peace with certain people, they make it extremely difficult. But you can be encouraged, knowing the Lord is not like us. Do not argue with anyone that is unreasonable, especially when you know they are not for peace but for drama and excitement. Have compassion upon yourself, and do what the Word of God commands you to do. Pray about it, and give the situation to the Lord. After you have done all you can, if whoever you are trying to make peace with still makes it impossible, then keep your peace.

The world is loaded with problems. When you turn on the television, most of the news is made up of trouble, sadness, death, scams, and evil. If you are familiar with the Word of God, this should not come as a surprise. Jesus told us, *"These things I have spoken unto you, that in me ye might have peace. In the world ye shall have tribulation: but be of good cheer; I have overcome the world"* (John 16:33, KJV).

THE PRINCE OF PEACE

Let me introduce you to the Prince of Peace, the Lord of all. There is a void in everyone's heart that only the Prince of Peace can fill. Once that void is filled, it becomes easier to find peace in life.

> *And the government shall be upon his shoulder: and his name shall be called Wonderful, Counsellor, The mighty God, The everlasting Father, The Prince of Peace."*
>
> ISAIAH 9:6, KJV

It is a peaceful feeling to know where you will spend eternity: *"For what shall it profit a man, if he shall gain the whole world, and lose his own soul? Or what shall a man give in exchange for his soul"* (Mark 8:36–37, KJV).

THE POWER OF COURAGEOUS FAITH 105

Now is the time to get yourself ready to meet God. Tomorrow may be too late. What are you waiting for? The Lord has opened the gate, and He is inviting you to come in: *"Jesus saith unto him, I am the way, the truth, and the life: no man cometh unto the Father, but by me"* (John 14:6–11, KJV).

Please take a few minutes and invite the Prince of Peace into your heart to fill that void in your life now. Here is a simple prayer for you to invite Him in:

> *Almighty God, thank You so much for sending Your only Son to die for my sins. Lord Jesus, I invite You into my heart now. I receive You as my Lord, Savior, and Prince of Peace. Please forgive my sins and show me how to live for You. Amen.*

It is important that you find a church where you can fellowship with other believers. Pray and ask the Lord to direct you to a Bible-believing church where you can learn sound biblical doctrine.

You can find peace in the Word of God. It is the will of God for you to have peace always:

> *Now the Lord of peace himself give you peace, always by all means. The Lord be with you all."*
>
> 2 THESSALONIANS 3:16, KJV

The Word of God tells us that God is for peace. Whenever Satan tries to mess with our peace, God fights for it. In fact, He has given this powerful promise: *"The God of peace shall bruise Satan under your feet shortly. The grace of our Lord Jesus Christ be with you. Amen"* (Romans 16:20, KJV).

PEACE IN KNOWING JESUS

It is the will of God for you to live a full, peaceful, and abundant life. The Word of God reveals the enemy's intention for your life and how the Lord Himself has already handled the situation:

> *The thief cometh not, but for to steal, and to kill, and to destroy I am come that they might have life, and that they might have it more abundantly."*
>
> JOHN 10:10, KJV

You must know that the enemy does not intend to leave you alone. He does not want you to have peace. He is invested in ensuring you have a miserable life filled with trouble, misfortune, tragedy, and failure. Satan delights in seeing children of God experience suffering. But praise be to God. The Lord did not leave you in darkness. He is a faithful God.

It is not the will of God for anyone to perish. There are rules and principles in place for you to follow to gain access to the true peace of God, and these rules are in the Bible. If you fail to follow the rules of life from God's Word, you give the enemy full control of your life: "*My people are destroyed for lack of knowledge*" (Hosea 4:6, KJV).

There is salvation and peace in knowing Jesus, who is the Lord of all:

> *Wherefore God also hath highly exalted him and given him a name which is above every name. That at the name of Jesus every knee should bow, of things in heaven, and things in earth, and things under the earth. And that every tongue should confess that Jesus Christ is Lord, to the glory of God the Father."*
>
> PHILIPPIANS 2:9–11, KJV

STAY ALERT AND MAINTAIN YOUR PEACE

A sober person is serious and thoughtful. A vigilant person is alert, awake, and watchful. You are not alone. The Lord wants you to be sober and vigilant to detect the enemy's lies and have peace.

> *Be sober, be vigilant; because your adversary the devil, as a roaring lion, walketh about, seeking whom he may devour: Whom resist steadfast in the faith, knowing that the same afflictions are accomplished in your brethren that are in the world."*
>
> 1 PETER 5:8–9, KJV

Although the enemy tries to do you wrong, guess what? God sees you as an overcomer. As John wrote in his epistle, *"Ye are of God, little children, and have overcome them: because greater is he that is in you, than he that is in the world"* (1 John 4:4, KJV). This is your true identity—overcomer!

My goal is to be effective in my journey as a Christian, psychotherapist, and counselor. I want to remain authentic in my relationship with God and my clients. I want to release peace to anyone that the Lord sends to cross my path. This peace is possible because Jesus gave us this promise: *"Peace I leave with you, my peace I give unto you: not as the world giveth, give I unto you. Let not your heart be troubled, neither let it be afraid"* (John 14:27, KJV).

LIVING A LIFE OF PEACE

For me, a life without peace is not worth living. Peace is a vital component to complete healthy living.

The devil does not want you to find peace. He is a pervert and will try to give you a counterfeit. Please do not make "peace" with the devil because he will tear your life to pieces and turn your life upside down. If you give the enemy access, you may never get your life back unless God intervenes.

One of the enemy's lies is that if you leave the devil alone, he will leave you alone. The truth, however, is that if you are God's child, the devil will never leave you alone. The Bible tells us that the devil is God's enemy. Be aware that your Father's enemy does not like you:

 Let God arise, let his enemies be scattered: let them also that hate him flee before him."

PSALM 68:1, KJV

INVEST TIME INTO GOD'S WORD

To have more peace, be familiar with God's Word. The Word of God allows you to function in line with the Holy Spirit. You receive supernatural answers to your questions, words of knowledge become natural occurrences, and it becomes more challenging for you to believe the lies of the enemy. Even in your silence, the Word of God is working for your good.

The Word of God is complete and has all the answers to the issues of this life. Make, find, and spend time in the presence of God and study His Word. The more you spend time studying God's Word, the more He reveals answers to your problems. Just as you withdraw funds from a bank account, you withdraw wisdom from your time spent in the Word. Likewise, when you study the Word of God, you save up for rainy days.

Similarly, just as a farmer sows his seed and reaps a harvest, in the same way, when you read or study the Word, you are sowing seeds. Expect to reap a bountiful harvest from your time spent studying the Bible. I encourage you to get the Bible app or access the Bible online.

If you do not feel like reading the Bible, use available resources to listen to the Word of God. It will enrich your spiritual life.

The enemy cannot stop you from listening to the Word. The most effective way to find peace in life is in the Word of God, where it is clear that nothing can separate you from His love and peace:

For I am persuaded, that neither death, nor life, nor angels, nor principalities, nor powers, nor things present, nor things to come. Nor height, nor depth, nor any other creature, shall be able to separate us from the love of God, which is in Christ Jesus our Lord."

ROMANS 8:38–39, KJV

Finding peace is possible when we do what the Lord commands:

And whatsoever ye do in word or deed, do all in the name of the Lord Jesus, giving thanks to God and the Father by him."

COLOSSIANS 3:17, KJV

God's plan for you is to have peace:

For I know the thoughts that I think toward you, saith the Lord, thoughts of peace, and not of evil, to give you an expected end."

JEREMIAH 29:11, KJV

The Lord wants you to have peace, always and by every means:

> *Now the Lord of peace himself gives you peace always by all means. The Lord be with you all."*
>
> 2 THESSALONIANS 3:16, KJV

The Word of God assures you that it is possible to have peace. Just like a little child reminds their father about what he had promised to give or do for them, you are free to remind God of His peace for you and accept the gift of love that He presents to you:

> *Yea, I have loved thee with an everlasting love: therefore with lovingkindness have I drawn thee."*
>
> JEREMIAH 31:3, KJV

Let the knowledge of God's Word and His love for you flood your heart, and it will invite the peace of God, which surpasses all understanding, to keep your heart and mind:

> *And the peace of God, which passeth all understanding, shall keep your hearts and minds through Christ Jesus."*
>
> PHILIPPIANS 4:7, KJV

When I realized the misery of a life without peace, I became intentional. I took time to pray for God to give me peace.

AN ENCOUNTER WITH THE SPIRIT OF PEACE

When Maggie and I started praying together, the Lord gave me wisdom, knowledge, and understanding on how to pray for peace in my life. He made me aware that as long as I live in this world, there will always be something to worry about, but if I follow what is in the Word of God, I can live life with peace.

Maggie applied what I learned about the source of peace to her life. She taught her children how to pray to God, specifically about their peace. They did, and she thanked me multiple times for sharing that information with her. I remind her that it is information found in the Bible, and she replies, "Give honor to whom honor is due."

When my son was born, my first prayer for him was that God would give him a life full of peace, according to this beautiful promise: *"And all thy children shall be taught of the Lord; and great shall be the peace of thy children"* (Isaiah 54:13, KJV).

When my son started talking, I taught Him how to pray for God's peace. We often ended our prayers with, "And great shall be our peace." I am not exempt from the cares of this world, but by the grace of God, I believe the Word of God, and I allow it to take root in my life. I also thank God for my earthly father, who taught me how to pray. When I have a specific need, I pray Scriptures over it and ask the Lord to keep me from evil, according to His Word:

Finally, brethren, pray for us, that the word of the Lord may have free course, and be glorified, even as it is with you. And that we may be delivered from unreasonable and wicked men: for all men have not faith. But the Lord is faithful, who shall stablish you, and keep you from evil."

2 THESSALONIANS 3:1–3, KJV

The Word of God is accurate and has been effective in my life. I encourage you to start or continue praying the Word of God over your life. Use Google to search for Scriptures that relate to your difficulties or concerns, and pray. When you pray the Word of God over your problems, the grace of God is made available to you by the Spirit of God.

And this is the confidence that we have in him, that, if we ask any thing according to his will, he heareth us. And if we know that he hears us, whatsoever we ask, we know that we have the petitions that we desired of him."

1 JOHN 5:14–16, KJV

SUMMARY

Peace is priceless. When you find peace, the enemy does not want you to keep it, so he tries as hard as he can to steal it. Only the Prince of Peace can fill the void in everyone's heart. Once that void is filled, it becomes easier to find peace in life. Receive the peace that the Lord offers you.

PRAYER

Lord, I choose to let the peace of God rule my heart and mind. Let me be intentional about allowing the Prince of Peace to take control of my life. Thank You, Lord, for giving me peace, always and by all means. Lord, I surrender all worries and uncomfortable feelings to You. Lord, I know Your plans for me are peaceful. Lord, fill my heart with Your peace as I fill it with Your Word. Lord, I ask for the peace of God, which surpasses all human understanding to keep my heart and mind. In Jesus's name, I pray. Amen.

DECLARATION OF FAITH

The Lord of Peace gives me peace all the time by all means. Amen.

ACTIVATION

- Ask the Lord to show you what is blocking the peace of God in your life.
- Ask the Lord to teach you how to acknowledge and maintain the peace of God in your life.
- Ask the Lord to help you live a surrendered life to the Prince of Peace.
- Ask the Lord to show you how to make the Prince of Peace the center of your life.
- Thank the Lord for giving you His best gift, Jesus.
- Ask the Lord to help you live a willing and faithful life for Jesus.
- Write down what you hear.

TEN
WHAT IS FEAR?

"I, even I, am he that comforteth you: who art thou, that thou shouldest be afraid of a man that shall die, and of the son of man which shall be made as grass. And forgettest the Lord thy maker, that hath stretched forth the heavens, and laid the foundations of the earth; and hast feared continually every day because of the fury of the oppressor, as if he were ready to destroy? and where is the fury of the oppressor?"
—Isaiah 51:12–13, KJV—

Fear is defined as "an unpleasant often strong emotion caused by anticipation or awareness of danger."[1] Fear is complicated. It is a game that Satan plays on people's minds, which can often feel real. In this chapter, we will discuss why you should be fearless. The Bible says, *"Be not afraid of sudden fear, neither of the desolation of the wicked, when it cometh"* (Proverbs 3:25, KJV).

THE POWER OF COURAGEOUS FAITH 115

The Lord commands that you should not fear:

 Fear thou not; for I am with thee: be not dismayed; for I am thy God: I will strengthen thee; yea, I will help thee; yea, I will uphold thee with the right hand of my righteousness."

ISAIAH 41:10, KJV

The enemy uses fear to afflict, terrorize, overwhelm, and torment individuals. If you give fear a second of your life, the spirit of fear will come in and completely take over. It then displays its negative attributes, such as anxiety, suspicion, doubt, judgment, and fear.

FEAR IS A SPIRIT

The Word of God calls fear a spirit:

 For God hath not given us the spirit of fear; but of power, and of love, and of a sound mind."

2 TIMOTHY 1:7, KJV

The spirit of fear is destructive and can torment you:

 There is no fear in love; but perfect love casteth out fear: because fear hath torment. He that feareth is not made perfect in love."

1 JOHN 4:18, KJV

The enemy uses the spirit of fear to remind you of your past failures. Fear can make you feel paralyzed whenever you try to revisit any project that you started, tested, and failed in the past. It steals your confidence in God, bullies, and magnifies the negative opinions of what the enemy wants you to hear. Instead of seeing the goodness of God in your life, the spirit of fear is readily available to pervert, counterfeit, and counteract God's Word that is meant to deliver you. The spirit of fear is a lion that roars loudly to get you running when no one is pursuing you. However, it is a clawless and toothless lion. It cannot harm you.

Before the Word of God delivered me from fear, I was tormented by it. In the middle of the night, I would become conscious but unable to move or talk, and I felt suffocated. I prayed in my mind. After much struggle, I would be able to stand up, pray, and confess the Word of God with wisdom, knowledge, and understanding. Fear left my life because of the power in God's Word.

I am committed to living and working by the principles of God's Word now. Because I did not know better before, I did not know how. Now I know better, and I do better. The Word of God assures me that God is with me, so I don't need to fear: *"Yea, though I walk through the valley of the shadow of death, I will fear no evil: for thou art with me; thy rod and thy staff they comfort me"* (Psalm 23:4, KJV).

ENCOUNTER WITH THE SPIRIT OF FEAR

I had many encounters with the spirit of fear. One night, as I stood in the kitchen, I felt overwhelmed and worried for no reason. It felt like the world was coming to an end. It was a bad feeling that words could not express. All I could remember was that I was in the fight, flight, freeze, or fawn mode. Walter Bradford Cannon, an American physiologist and professor, calls this hyperarousal or the acute stress response. It is a physiological reaction that occurs in response to a perceived harmful event, attack, or threat to survival.[2] As indicated by Gozhenko and his colleagues, this response is recognized as the first stage of the general adaptation syndrome that regulates stress responses among vertebrates and other organisms.[3] It is real to the person experiencing fear. I was frozen for a few seconds, and then the flight took over. I ran from the kitchen to the living room and fell on my knees on my couch. When I prayed, I experienced the peace of God.

If the spirit of fear attacks you, pray and call upon God. The spirit of fear is no match to the spirit of prayer.

VICTORY OVER THE SPIRIT OF FEAR

I got victory over the spirit of fear when I started spending more time with the Lord in prayer and the Word of God. The day I was delivered, I had a dream. I saw many funny and ugly creatures running toward me. When I turned to look at the creatures, I blew at them, and the breath from my mouth was so powerful that it knocked the creatures back. When I woke up, I knew something had happened in the spirit realm. That dream increased my confidence in the Lord.

But the spirit of fear did not give up. The straw that broke the camel's back was another encounter in my bedroom. This time, the spirit of fear was surprised and never returned. I had grown in the spirit and knowledge of the Word of God.

On this particular night, I was fast asleep in my bedroom. Suddenly, I woke up from a deep sleep. I saw a giant black figure standing at the door of my bedroom. I give God all the glory for how I reacted to that giant dark figure. I turned over on my side and pulled the comforter over my head. I did not say a word. I went right back to sleep. I was not afraid of the terror by night. When you spend time in the presence of God, the Bible promises, *"Thou shalt not be afraid for the terror by night"* (Psalm 91:5, KJV). I was overwhelmed by the spirit of peace when I woke up in the morning. I praised and worshiped the Lord for such a breathtaking encounter with the living God.

It is too late; nobody can convince me now or at any other time that there is no God. That night, the spirit of fear discovered that the greater One dwells in me:

Greater is he that is in you than he that is in the world."

1 JOHN 4:4, KJV

Whenever you experience fear, pray and speak the Word of God over the situation. Remember that God will honor His Word:

Have not I commanded thee? Be strong and of a good courage; be not afraid, neither be thou dismayed: for the Lord thy God is with thee whithersoever thou goest."

JOSHUA 1:9, KJV

Another way the spirit of fear intimidates is through communication. As the fire begins to burn, you control the degree to which the fire progresses or diminishes.

If you respond negatively, the enemy pours more gasoline. Your negative response empowers the enemy to take over the situation. Be encouraged in your faith, trust the Lord, and be convinced that God is good. Be not afraid:

Say to them that are of a fearful heart, Be strong, fear not: behold, your God will come with vengeance, even God with a recompence; he will come and save you."

ISAIAH 35:4, KJV

Be like Paul, who was deeply convinced about his faith. Paul had several encounters with the spirit of fear. Paul was not even afraid of the spirit of death; he trusted God. Paul wrote:

For to me to live is Christ, and to die is gain. But if I live in the flesh, this is the fruit of my labour: yet what I shall

choose I wot not. For I am in a strait betwixt two, having a desire to depart, and to be with Christ, which is far better."

PHILIPPIANS 1:21–23, KJV

Remember, the enemy will not take it easy with you. He is on a mission to destroy, and his master key is the spirit of fear. Ask the Lord to deliver you from fear. Fear had to go for me to function effectively. One can only give to others what they have, and I refuse to transfer the spirit of fear to others:

 For God hath not given us the spirit of fear; but of power, and of love, and of a sound mind."

2 TIMOTHY 1:7, KJV

As you seek God more deeply and sincerely, the enemy will fight. But remember you are blessed:

 Blessed be the God and Father of our Lord Jesus Christ, who hath blessed us with all spiritual blessings in heavenly places in Christ."

EPHESIANS 1:3, KJV

The enemy will never hand over anything to you peacefully. Take your peace by force from the enemy:

 And from the days of John the Baptist until now, the kingdom of heaven suffereth violence, and the violent take it by force."

MATTHEW 11:12, KJV

You can live a fear-free life when you walk by faith:

> *For we walk by faith, not by sight."*
>
> 2 CORINTHIANS 5:7, KJV

You cannot do it by yourself but by God's ability:

> *Not by might, nor by power, but by my spirit, saith the Lord of hosts."*
>
> ZECHARIAH 4:6, KJV

Fear is a stronghold. Because it works in your mind, cast out all demonic thoughts. Fight fear from the spiritual realm, and use God's Word to cast fear out. Fear tends to exalt itself against the knowledge of God. You have to bring fear into captivity:

> *Casting down imaginations, and every high thing that exalteth itself against the knowledge of God and bringing into captivity every thought to the obedience of Christ."*
>
> 2 CORINTHIANS 10:5–7, KJV

HOW TO WAGE WAR ON THE SPIRIT OF FEAR

I attack fear with prayer, praise, the Word, and worship. I dance before the Lord with joy, more in private than in public, and I do it often. I am not ashamed of my Lord. It does not matter what fear says.

When I wake up, I dance before the Lord.

For I am not ashamed of the gospel of Christ: for it is the power of God unto salvation to everyone that believeth."

ROMANS 1:16, KJV

I am convinced that whatever the enemy presents to me in the form of fear is seeking for my worship. If a situation causes me to feel fearful, I place that situation before God, releasing it to Him, and worship. Whatever tries to steal your joy or peace must be summoned to the place of worship. They must all participate in giving glory to the Lord. It works for me. The more you spend time in prayer, the more you get closer to God and the less fear you experience: *"Draw nigh to God, and he will draw nigh to you"* (James 4:8, KJV).

GOD COMFORTED ME IN A DREAM BEFORE THE PANDEMIC

Before COVID-19, I spent plenty of time in God's presence. One night, I had a dream. I was walking alone on a bridge. On both sides of the bridge, dead bodies were floating in the river. As I walked on the bridge, I meditated on Psalm 91, which comforted me. The Lord encouraged me not to fear. Through the entire pandemic, I did not experience any form of fear. When the pandemic got difficult, the Lord reminded me of the dream and encouraged me to pray Psalm 91. My dear friend, fear not; God is real. He keeps His word.

THE SPIRIT OF FEAR WANTS YOUR WORSHIP

This is what I received from the Lord about the spirit of fear. While waiting at a traffic light one day, I heard: When you pray, praise, worship, and read God's Word, you displace fear in your mind. The spirit of joy flows freely into your heart and mind. You must be aware that the enemy is a pervert, and allowing fear to overwhelm your life makes the enemy happy. The enemy is delighted when you are full of fear because he can manipulate better and easier. The enemy is a wicked taskmaster who does not allow his followers to have peace. Anytime you catch yourself fearful, change it to praise and worship of your Savior, the Lord Jesus Christ. It will send the enemy running.

THE FEAR OF THE LORD

The fear of the Lord differs from the intense emotion caused by anticipation or awareness of danger.

Instead, when you have the fear of God, you begin to have God's wisdom, knowledge, understanding, and long life:

> *The fear of the Lord is the beginning of wisdom: and the knowledge of the holy is understanding. For by me thy days shall be multiplied, and the years of thy life shall be increased. If thou be wise, thou shalt be wise for thyself: but if thou scornest, thou alone shalt bear it."*
>
> PROVERBS 9:10–12, KJV

When you have the fear of God, you can abstain from sin:

> *And Moses said unto the people, Fear not: for God is come to prove you, and that his fear may be before your faces, that ye sin not."*
>
> EXODUS 20:20, KJV

To fear the Lord is to revere Him. Keep His commandments always, and when you fear God, it shall be well with you and your children:

O that there were such an heart in them, that they would fear me, and keep all my commandments always, that it might be well with them, and with their children for ever."

DEUTERONOMY 5:29, KJV

The fear of the Lord is to receive His words, obey His commandments, seek the wisdom and understanding of God, and know Him:

My son, if thou wilt receive my words, and hide my commandments with thee; So that thou incline thine ear unto wisdom, and apply thine heart to understanding; Yea, if thou criest after knowledge, and liftest up thy voice for understanding; If thou seekest her as silver, and searchest for her as for hid treasures. Then shalt thou understand the fear of the Lord and find the knowledge of God."

PROVERBS 2:1–5, KJV

The Word of God commands:

Honor all men. Love the brotherhood. Fear God. Honor the king."

1 PETER 2:17, KJV

The Lord hates evil. When you fear the Lord, you should do likewise:

The fear of the Lord is to hate evil: pride, and arrogancy, and the evil way, and the froward mouth, do I hate."

PROVERBS 8:13, KJV

SUMMARY

Dear saint, you must know the differences between the spirit of fear and the fear of the Lord. Fear has tormenting power. But, when you draw near to the Lord, He promises to give you the spirit of power, love, and a sound mind. Instead of allowing the enemy to torment you with his spirit of fear, you should cultivate the spirit of the fear of God that gives wisdom, knowledge, and understanding.

PRAYER

Lord, You are my shepherd, and I shall not want. Lord, I choose to believe Your Word. I will fear no evil, for You are with me. Thy rod and staff comfort me. Lord, I refuse to worry. I know that You are with me. I am not dismayed, for I know that You are my God. Lord, You strengthen, help, and uphold me with Your righteous right hand. Lord, I bless You. I am an overcomer because greater is He that is in me than he that is in the world. Lord, I thank You as I put my hand in Your hand and take this new journey of life with no fear. And Lord, thank You for giving me the spirit of power, love, and a sound mind. As I seek you, Lord, You hear and deliver me from all my fears. In Jesus's name, I pray. Amen.

DECLARATION OF FAITH

The Lord is my light and my salvation; whom shall I fear? The Lord is the strength of my life; of whom shall I be afraid?"

PSALM 27:1, KJV

ACTIVATION

- Ask the Lord to show you how to deal with the spirit of fear.
- Ask the Lord to show you the root cause of fear in your life.
- Ask the Lord to teach you how to use prayer, praise, the Word, and worship to wage war against the spirit of fear.
- Ask the Lord to reveal the fear of the Lord, which is the beginning of wisdom, knowledge, and understanding.
- Ask the Lord to teach you to fear His face so you do not sin.
- Thank the Lord as He multiplies your years and gives you divine health as you honor and fear Him.
- Write down what you hear.

ELEVEN
DELIVERANCE FROM THE ENEMY

> *"And it shall come to pass, that whosoever shall call on the name of the Lord shall be delivered: for in mount Zion and in Jerusalem shall be deliverance, as the Lord hath said, and in the remnant whom the Lord shall call."*
> —Joel 2:32, KJV—

Deliverance means to be rescued from a specific situation or circumstance. Deliverance from the enemy is rescue from demonic oppression or possession. The components for obtaining deliverance are the Word of God, the name of the Lord, and the blood of Jesus. I will discuss the Bible and personal stories about deliverance. In addition, we will explore how to obtain and maintain your deliverance from the enemy using God's Word. The good news is that your full deliverance is possible when you call upon the name of the Lord.

DELIVERANCE FOR THE HOUSE OF JACOB

Pharaoh had a dream from God. God used Joseph, the dreamer, to interpret His messages to Pharaoh. In his dream, Pharaoh saw seven fat cows and seven lean cows, and the seven fat cows swallowed the seven lean ones. He had a second dream. This time, he saw seven ears of corn. There were seven thin ears of corn and seven good-looking ears of corn, and the seven thin ears devoured the seven full ears. When he awoke in the morning, his spirit was troubled. Joseph interpreted Pharaoh's dreams:

> *And Joseph said unto Pharaoh, the dream of Pharaoh is one: God hath shewed Pharaoh what he is about to do. The seven good kine are seven years; and the seven good ears are seven years: the dream is one. And the seven thin and ill-favcred kine that came up after them are seven years; and the seven empty ears blasted with the east wind shall be seven years of famine."*
>
> GENESIS 41:25–27, KJV

Years before, Joseph's brothers had sold him to the Ishmaelites. The God who knows the end of things from the beginning allowed this in preparation for the famine. Joseph's interpretation of Pharaoh's dream landed him a job as the second in command. When the famine manifested, Jacob became aware of bread in Egypt and sent his sons there.

When Joseph's brothers met face-to-face with him in Egypt, Joseph forgave them and assured them that it was all according to God's plan. While God's intention was incomprehensible to man, it brought deliverance to the tribe of Jacob.

God brought deliverance to Jacob through Joseph. The Lord revealed to Joseph what would happen to him in the future in his dream, but

Joseph could not understand why all the harmful things were happening to him. The good news is that the Lord knows the end from the beginning. Joseph's destiny was to preserve Israel, and God settled this assignment from the start of his life.

Just like Joseph, the Lamb of God was slain from the foundation of the world to deliver humankind, and the Lord was pleased with Jesus from the beginning:

> *He shall see of the travail of his soul and shall be satisfied: by his knowledge shall my righteous servant justify many; for he shall bear their iniquities."*

ISAIAH 53:11, KJV

If you are battling with failure and disappointment, I encourage you to seek answers from God. Trust the process. The all-knowing God is working to bring you deliverance. Do not fight the process. Instead, use the weapons of your warfare discussed in the previous chapters while you wait. Be reminded that your God is fighting your battles behind the scenes, and your God will deliver you:

> *Behold, I will send my messenger, and he shall prepare the way before me: and the Lord, whom ye seek, shall suddenly come to his temple, even the messenger of the covenant, whom ye delight in behold, he shall come, saith the Lord of hosts."*

MALACHI 3:3, KJV

THE PRICE OF DELIVERANCE FOR ISRAEL AND HUMANITY

Although Joseph's brothers sold him to the Ishmeelites for twenty pieces of silver, God used it to preserve His people from famine:

Come, and let us sell him to the Ishmeelites, and let not our hand be upon him, for he is our brother and our flesh. And his brethren were content. Then there passed by Midianites merchantmen; they drew and lifted Joseph out of the pit and sold Joseph to the Ishmeelites for twenty pieces of silver: and they brought Joseph into Egypt."

GENESIS 37:26–28, KJV

Likewise, although Judas betrayed Jesus, God worked it out for good:

Judas Iscariot, went unto the chief priests, and said unto them, what will ye give me, and I will deliver him unto you? And they covenanted with him for thirty pieces of silver."

MATTHEW 26:14–15, KJV

THE WORD OF GOD DELIVERS

The Word of God has been there from the start:

In the beginning was the Word, and the Word was with God, and the Word was God."

JOHN 1:1, KJV

The Lord made everything with His Word. *"In the beginning, God created the heaven and the earth"* (Genesis 1:1, KJV). The Lord also upholds and controls everything by the Word of His power:

> *Who being the brightness of his glory, and the express image of his person, and upholding all things by the word of his power, when he had by himself purged our sins, sat down on the right hand of the Majesty on high."*
>
> HEBREWS 1:3, KJV

The Bible shows us that the Word of God delivers:

> *He sent his word, and healed them, and delivered them from their destruction."*
>
> PSALM 107:20, KJV

The Word of God declares salvation from God:

> *He that is our God is the God of salvation; and unto God the Lord belong the issues from death."*
>
> PSALM 68:20, KJV

The Word declares God encompasses you with songs of deliverance:

> *Thou art my hiding place; thou shalt preserve me from trouble; thou shalt compass me about with songs of deliverance. Selah. I will instruct thee and teach thee in the way which thou shalt go I will guide thee with mine eye."*
>
> PSALM 32:7–8, KJV

THE POWER OF COURAGEOUS FAITH

God promised Abraham to deliver Israel in His Word:

> *And he said unto Abram, Know of a surety that thy seed shall be a stranger in a land that is not theirs, and shall serve them; and they shall afflict them four hundred years. And also, that nation, whom they shall serve, will I judge and afterward shall they come out with great substance."*
>
> GENESIS 15:13–14, KJV

GOD PRESERVED AND DELIVERED ISRAEL BY HIS WORD

The Lord sent Joseph to Egypt to preserve the tribe of Jacob from hunger and extinction. Then God convinced Jacob that Joseph was alive and that he should not be afraid to go down to Egypt:

> *And God Spake unto Israel in the visions of the night, and said, Jacob, Jacob. And he said, here am I. And he said I am God, the God of thy Father: fear not to go down into Egypt; for I will there make of thee a great nation."*
>
> GENESIS 46:2–3, KJV

The Lord preserved Moses to witness the affliction of the Israelites by Pharoah and used him to bring them out of slavery:

> *Therefore, they did set over them taskmasters to afflict them with their burdens. And they built for Pharaoh treasure cities, Pithom and Raamses."*
>
> EXODUS 1:11, KJV

Pharaoh oppressed the children of Israel. When they cried out to God, He heard them:

> *Wherefore say unto the children of Israel, I am the Lord, and I will bring you out from under the burdens of the Egyptians, and I will rid you out of their bondage, and I will redeem you with a stretched-out arm, and with great judgments."*
>
> EXODUS 6:6, KJV

While Pharaoh ordered the killings of all the male children of the Jews, God sent Moses to deliver them from bondage:

> *Now therefore, behold, the cry of the children of Israel is come unto me: and I have also seen the oppression wherewith the Egyptians oppress them. Come now therefore, and I will send thee unto Pharaoh, that thou mayest bring forth my people the children of Israel out of Egypt."*
>
> EXODUS 3:9—10, KJV

Afterward, the Lord sent Moses to deliver Israel from slavery by the Egyptians. Moses led the people across the Red Sea:

> *And Moses said unto the people, Fear ye not, stand still, and see the salvation of the Lord, which he will shew to you today: for the Egyptians whom ye have seen today, ye shall see them again no more forever."*
>
> EXODUS 14:13, KJV

Similar to Pharaoh, Herod ordered the killings of all the male children of the Jews, but God preserved Jesus to deliver humanity:

> *Behold, the angel of the Lord appeareth to Joseph in a dream, saying, Arise, and take the young child and his mother, and flee into Egypt, and be thou there until I bring thee word: for Herod will seek the young child to destroy him."*
>
> MATTHEW 2:13, KJV

DELIVERANCE IS IN THE NAME AND BLOOD OF JESUS

Jesus delivered you from the power of darkness into the Kingdom of Jesus:

> *Who hath delivered us from the power of darkness, and hath translated us into the kingdom of his dear Son."*
>
> COLOSSIANS 1:13, KJV

Your salvation is in the name of Jesus:

> *Neither is there salvation in any other: for there is none other name under heaven given among men, whereby we must be saved."*
>
> ACTS 4:12, KJV

In the name of Jesus, you can cast out devils:

> *And these signs shall follow them that believe; In my name shall they cast out devils; they shall speak with new*

tongues. They shall take up serpents; and if they drink any deadly thing, it shall not hurt them; they shall lay hands on the sick, and they shall recover."

MARK 16:17–18, KJV

There was silence in Heaven for half an hour because no one was worthy of taking up the responsibility of dying to save humanity: *"And no man in heaven, nor in earth, neither under the earth, was able to open the book, neither to look thereon"* (Revelation 5:3, KJV). But all glory to God. The Lord Jesus stepped up, and willingly, He unsealed the book:

Thou art worthy to take the book, and to open the seals thereof: for thou wast slain, and hast redeemed us to God by thy blood out of every kindred, and tongue, and people, and nation."

REVELATION 5:9, KJV

The shed blood of Jesus legalized the reconciliation for sin: *"And, having made peace through the blood of his cross, by him to reconcile all things unto himself; by him, I say, whether they be things in earth, or things in heaven"* (Colossians 1:20, KJV).

MAINTAIN YOUR DELIVERANCE

To maintain your deliverance, you must put on the whole armor of God, which includes:

- Belt of Truth
- Breastplate of righteousness
- Gospel of peace
- Shield of faith

- Helmet of salvation
- Sword of the Spirit, which is the Word of God
- Perseverance and supplication for all saints

Wherefore take unto you the whole armour of God, that ye may be able to withstand in the evil day, and having done all, to stand. Stand therefore, having your loins girt about with truth, and having on the breastplate of righteousness; And your feet shod with the preparation of the gospel of peace. Above all, taking the shield of faith, wherewith ye shall be able to quench all the fiery darts of the wicked. And take the helmet of salvation and the sword of the Spirit, the Word of God. Praying always with all prayer and supplication in the Spirit and watching thereunto with all perseverance and supplication for all saints."

EPHESIANS 6:13–18, KJV

DELIVERANCE FOR MY PRAYER PARTNER'S DAUGHTER

Maggie, who was barren for eighteen years, was blessed with her first daughter after we prayed. When it was time for her daughter to go to college, the enemy inflicted her with the spirit of anxiety and depression. She was troubled by fear, anxiety, depression, and panic attacks. She pleaded with her mother to get her out of the dormitory. When Maggie brought her home, things became dire and complicated.

Whenever Maggie called her daughter on her cellphone, she would not answer. She told her mother that when her mother called her, she would lay in bed and look at the phone. She indicated that she did not want to answer her mother's calls. I decided to visit her. I called her, but she did not pick up. I parked my car in front of her house, and when I got to her room, she looked at the phone on her bed. She refused to talk to me. When I got back to my car, I had a parking ticket. I knew there was war. Maggie and I did not give up. We held on to the Word of God and continued to pray.

Although things were not looking good, God was working behind the scenes.

We confessed God's Word, prayed, praised, gave thanks, and worshiped as we waited on God for victory. We had a breakthrough. God surprised all of us. The young lady started improving from the state of depression the enemy had placed her in. Today, that once fearful young lady, who lived in severe anxiety and depression, is now an air hostess, flying around the world fearlessly. She is also in school. Hallelujah!

God said to call on Him in our time of trouble: *"And call upon me in the day of trouble: I will deliver thee, and thou shalt glorify me"* (Psalm 50:15, KJV). We called, and He answered.

ONLY JESUS CAN DELIVER

Jesus rescued humanity from the grip of Satan with His shed blood. He conquered Satan. Deliverance is God's will for you. Jesus came to set you free from every bondage of Satan. The Lord has given you the authority to overcome the enemy:

> *See, I have this day set thee over the nations and the kingdoms, to root out, and to pull down, and to destroy, and to throw down, to build, and to plant."*
>
> JEREMIAH 1:10, KJV

You have power over serpents and scorpions:

> *Behold, I give unto you power to tread on serpents and scorpions, and over all the power of the enemy: and nothing shall by any means hurt you."*
>
> LUKE 10:19, KJV

In the name of Jesus, Paul cast out a demon from a woman who possessed a spirit of divination:

> *The same followed Paul and us, and cried, saying, these men are the servants of the most high God, which shew unto us the way of salvation. And this did she many days. But Paul, being grieved, turned and said to the Spirit, I command thee in the name of Jesus Christ to come out of her. And he came out the same hour."*
>
> ACTS 16:17–18, KJV

The name of Jesus is powerful and can deliver those who are possessed with demonic power.

THE LAWFUL CAPTIVE DELIVERED

The Lord reminds us in His Word that He can deliver lawful captives from their enemies: *"Shall the prey be taken from the mighty, or the lawful captive delivered? But thus saith the Lord, Even the captives of the mighty shall be taken away, and the prey of the terrible shall be delivered: for I will contend with him that contendeth with thee, and I will save thy children"* (Isaiah 49:24–25, KJV).

Dear saint, even when you are legally or lawfully liable for judgment against you, do not give up. Trust God. Call upon Him, and remind Him of His Word.

Then they cried unto the Lord in their trouble, and he delivered them out of their distresses."

PSALM 107:6, KJV

Are you troubled? Remember, Jesus Christ is Lord: *"If the son therefore shall make you free, ye shall be free indeed"* (John 8:36, KJV).

The Lord Jesus went to the cross to save you from the enemy's works: *"I am the good shepherd: the good shepherd giveth his life for the sheep"* (John 10:11, KJV).

SUMMARY

The Lord promised to deliver you from the enemy through the Word of God, the name of the Lord, and the blood of Jesus. After you have been delivered, it is important that you maintain your deliverance. You maintain your deliverance when you know what the Word of God teaches about it. Call upon the Lord, and be delivered.

PRAYER

Lord, I choose to call upon You to deliver me from trouble. Thank You, Lord, for fighting my battles. Thank You, Lord Jesus, for Your shed blood. Lord, lead me not into temptation but deliver me from evil. Thank You, Lord; You are my rock, fortress, and deliverer. Lord, I thank You for delivering me from the power of darkness and translating me into the Kingdom of Your dear Son. Lord, I receive power to tread on serpents and scorpions and over all the power of the enemy. I thank You, Lord, for nothing shall by any means hurt me.

DECLARATION OF FAITH

He sent His Word, and He healed and delivered me from my destruction.

ACTIVATION

- Take some time to call on the name of the Lord, and ask Him to deliver you.
- Remind the Lord that He said there shall be deliverance.[1]
- Take some time in prayer, and ask the Lord to show you what to let go of in your life that is blocking the Holy Spirit's free access. This could be doubt, unbelief, or more.
- Ask the Lord to show you areas that need deliverance from the enemy, such as addiction from food, substances, or bitterness against someone.
- Ask the Lord to deliver you from oppression or possession by the enemy.
- Ask the Lord to reveal open doors that give the enemy access into your life.
- Ask the Lord to teach you not to be afraid but to stand still and see the salvation of the Lord in your life.
- Thank the Lord, for it is the will of God that you receive deliverance.
- Write down what you hear.

TWELVE
WHERE IS GOD WHEN THINGS ARE GOING WRONG?

> *"When you pass through the waters,
> I will be with you, And through the rivers,
> they shall not overflow you. When you walk
> through the fire, you shall not be burned,
> nor shall the flame scorch you."*
> —**Isaiah 43:2, NKJV**—

Do you feel stuck in a cycle of never-ending difficulty? The love of God for you—in any and every circumstance—is promised in His Word. God remains faithful to His Word. Whatever your story is, God can make it right for you. God can give you the grace to bear any burden.

I encourage you to open your heart and let the Lord comfort you with His Word. God said He will make a way for you. I encourage you to trust the Lord.

Behold, I will do a new thing; now it shall spring forth; shall ye not know it? I will even make a way in the wilderness, and rivers in the desert."

ISAIAH 43:19, KJV

When you experience inconvenient situations, God is with you: *"God is our refuge and strength, a very present help in trouble"* (Psalm 46:1, KJV). As you read this chapter, healing will take place.

If you struggle to forgive those who hurt you, I encourage you to give it to the Lord. He promised He would repay: *"Dearly beloved, avenge not yourselves, but rather give place unto wrath: for it is written, Vengeance is mine; I will repay, saith the Lord"* (Romans 12:19, KJV).

The Lord promises that He will not leave or forsake you. Trust and believe that He cares for you.

GOD CARES ABOUT YOU

God is faithful to His Word. Let the Lord wrap His loving arms around you. Place your head on His chest or shoulder, and let God's love comfort you: *"I have loved thee with an everlasting love; therefore, with lovingkindness have I drawn thee"* (Jeremiah 31:3, KJV).

If you did not have basic amenities growing up or are an orphan, be hopeful because God is faithful. He will make it up to you. If you do not have fond memories of your childhood or did not receive the same kind of love your friends did, know that God loves you. Lamentations 3:22–23 says, *"The steadfast love of the Lord never ceases; His mercies never come to an end; they are new every morning; great is your faithfulness."* It is well. God is still a loving Father.

If you did not have friends growing up or feel lonely and depressed now, do not be discouraged. He is a good friend. He will give you joy and strengthen you in tough times: *"My flesh and my heart faileth: but*

God is the strength of my heart, and my portion forever" (Psalm 73:26, KJV).

God cares for you, and He loves you. Give the Word of God access to your heart. God is knocking at the door of your heart, and He wants to embrace you. Will you let Him? He is still in the business of answering prayers. Talk to Him. Open your heart, and receive His love.

> *Cause me to hear thy lovingkindness in the morning; for in thee do I trust cause me to know the way wherein I should walk; for I lift up my soul unto thee."*
>
> PSALM 143:8, KJV

RIDICULED AND ABANDONED BY FAMILY AND FRIENDS

Perhaps your classmates made fun of you for wearing the same clothes most days of the week to school as a child. You had no friends, and people avoided you. Your teachers did not like you, and you did not like yourself. Your biological parents neglected you, and foster parents and students did not want you in their company. Have confidence in God. He can make things right for you:

> *Cast not away therefore your confidence, which hath great recompence of reward. For ye have need of patience, that, after ye have done the will of God, ye might receive the promise."*
>
> HEBREWS 10:35–36, KJV

Perhaps your mother or father abandoned you mentally, emotionally, or physically, or they were more interested in their career than in you. Perhaps they were addicted to drugs, alcohol, or both, and they left you alone. You were raised by your siblings, grandparents, uncles, aunties, or their friends, leaving you in danger of those who did not care about your safety.

Perhaps your parents never said they loved you. The people who were supposed to protect you sexually abused you. You ended up in foster homes because no one in your family wanted you. You did not complete or attend high school because of a lack of counsel. Perhaps you are an immigrant, and all your family members live abroad.

Perhaps you are married but feel very much alone. You live with a spouse who abuses you emotionally, psychologically, or physically and gives you daily doses of silent treatment.

Or perhaps you are in a relationship and live together, but he refuses to marry you. The doctor has diagnosed you with a terrible disease. You are a new mother who is too sick to care for your newborn. You are a pregnant teenager; your parents demand you give away your newborn for adoption. You do not have a job, cannot find a job in your field, or are too sick to work. You were illegally trafficked for sexual purposes, are still in it, and need help to get out. The person or people who should have protected you from harm raped you multiple times, or others raped you. You have no permission to work because of a visa issue. You are battling with a combination of mental and physical health issues. You cry and self-medicate with drugs or alcohol.

Even if one or more of those painful difficulties I have listed may be your reality, please be aware that God is good. He is faithful and able to deliver those who trust in Him.

Many are the afflictions of the righteous: but the Lord delivereth him out of them all."

PSALM 34:19, KJV

It would be best if you did not allow the enemy to use what you have been through to torment you. Wherever life has taken you, remember that God is on your side.

What shall we then say to these things? If God be for us, who can be against us? He that spared not his own Son, but delivered him up for us all, how shall he not with him also freely give us all things."

ROMANS 8:31–39, KJV

COMFORT FOR THE OVERWHELMED HEART

When I feel overwhelmed, I run to the rock of my salvation. When I do not want to pray or praise the Lord, I walk and listen to the Word of God on audio. The enemy cannot stop you from hearing the Word. I listen to music that glorifies the Lord, and before my walk ends, I feel better. When you are overwhelmed, I encourage you to take a praise break:

I will love thee, O Lord, my strength. The Lord is my rock, and my fortress, and my deliverer; my God, my strength, in whom I will trust; my buckler, and the horn of my salvation, and my high tower."

PSALM 18:1–2, KJV

It is helpful to run to the Lord when things get tough and you don't know what else to do. Ask the Lord to hear your cry, and let His mercy and truth preserve you:

Hear my cry, O God; attend unto my prayer. From the end of the earth will I cry unto thee, when my heart is overwhelmed: lead me to the rock that is higher than I. For thou

hast been a shelter for me, and a strong tower from the enemy."

PSALM 61:1–3, KJV

Have confidence in the Lord, be courageous, and let God's Word comfort you. If your heart condemns you, turn to the Word of God. It is more reliable than your feelings:

And hereby we know that we are of the truth and shall assure our hearts before him. For if our heart condemns us, God is greater than our heart, and knoweth all things. Beloved, if our heart condemns us not, then have we confidence toward God. And whatsoever we ask, we receive of him, because we keep his commandments, and do those things that are pleasing in his sight."

1 JOHN 3:19–22, KJV

When you go through tough times, the Lord doesn't want you to be ashamed; He wants you to believe in Him. He can answer your prayer:

For the which cause I also suffer these things: nevertheless, I am not ashamed: for I know whom I have believed and am persuaded that he is able to keep that which I have committed unto him against that day."

2 TIMOTHY 1:12, KJV

The Lord corrects us to give us peace, and healing will come as we obey.

Arise and welcome God's healing presence into your life.

> *Now no chastening seems to be joyful for the present, but painful; nevertheless, afterward it yields the peaceable fruit of righteousness to those who have been trained by it. Therefore, strengthen the hands which hang down, and the feeble knees, and make straight paths for your feet, so that what is lame may not be dislocated, but rather be healed."*
>
> HEBREWS 12:11–13, NKJV

The Lord is faithful. I encourage you to hold fast to your faith, and love the Lord through every trial you face:

> *Let us draw near with a true heart in full assurance of faith, having our hearts sprinkled from an evil conscience, and our bodies washed with pure water. Let us hold fast the profession of our faith without wavering; for he is faithful that promised; And let us consider one another to provoke unto love and to good works."*
>
> HEBREWS 10:22–25, KJV

CONSIDER GETTING PROFESSIONAL HELP

If you have or are experiencing any of the above issues, please get professional help for your mental or physical well-being. Son or daughter of God, nurture your spirit by spending and enjoying quality time with the Holy Spirit. You should be mindful not to neglect your relationship with the Lord.

The Lord gave wisdom to professionals to help people navigate the trials of life. Get help for your mental health challenges if you need to. And as you do, continue to trust God for His divine help because nothing is too complicated for the Lord:

Ah Lord God! Behold, thou hast made the heaven and the earth by Thy great power and outstretched arm; and there is nothing too hard for Thee."

JEREMIAH 32:17, KJV

DAVID, A MAN AFTER GOD'S HEART

In 2 Samuel 6, David begged King Saul to permit him to deal with Goliath for defying the armies of the living God. King David had challenging times. David's father separated him as a young boy from his family to keep his father's sheep in the wilderness. After David slew the giant, King Saul was jealous and tried to kill David. When David returned from the slaughter of the Philistine, women came from every city of Israel, singing and dancing: *"And the women answered one another as they played, and said, Saul hath slain his thousands, and David his ten thousands"* (1 Samuel 18:7, KJV).

King Saul was displeased that they ascribed unto David ten thousands, and to him they ascribed but thousands. Because of this, *"Saul eyed David from that day and forward"* (1 Samuel 18:9, KJV). David prayed to God to protect his life, and He delivered David. David glorified God for His love for him. *"And he said, The Lord is my rock, and my fortress, and my deliverer"* (2 Samuel 22:1–2, KJV).

David experienced grim times, but God called David a man after His own heart. The Lord took away the kingdom from King Saul and gave it to David:

 But now thy kingdom shall not continue: the Lord hath sought him a man after his own heart, and the Lord hath commanded him to be captain over his people, because thou hast not kept that which the Lord commanded thee."

1 SAMUEL 13:14, KJV

After David became a king, he faced even more challenges. By this time, he was prepared; he had mastered the craft of seeking and getting God's attention: *"And David was greatly distressed; for the people spake of stoning him, because the soul of all the people was grieved, every man for his sons and for his daughters: but David encouraged himself in the Lord his God"* (1 Samuel 30:6, KJV).

You should read the Word, pray, praise, and worship the Lord in spirit and truth. Do what David did when he was in serious trouble. Could the Lord have something for you in the future like He had for David? Draw closer to the Lord when you get troubled with the issues of this life, just as we are encouraged in this Scripture: *"Draw nigh to God, and he will draw nigh to you"* (James 4:8, KJV).

PRAY FOR THOSE IN NEED

If you are not affected by the above challenges or cannot relate to them, to God be the glory. Say a short prayer for any of your brothers, sisters, family members, or loved ones who are affected. Allow the Holy Spirit to use you as God's hands and feet to accomplish His work on earth. Ask God to give you empathy, grace, and mercy for those in need of help: *"Wherefore comfort yourselves together and edify one another"* (1 Thessalonians 5:11, KJV).

GIVE YOURSELF A BREAK

When was the last time you took a break? If you can, and if it is possible, you should take some time off to rest, reflect, and be in God's presence. If you can, step out into nature and discover the beauty of God's creation: *"The Lord covers heaven with clouds, he prepares rain for the earth, and makes grass to grow on the mountains"* (Psalm 147:8, NKJV).

Take time to admire the flowers and smell the roses:

Consider the lilies, how they grow: they neither toil nor spin; and yet I say to you, even Solomon in all his glory was not arrayed like one of these. If then God so clothes the grass, which today is in the field and tomorrow is thrown into the oven, how much more will He clothe you."

LUKE 12:27–28, KJV

I pray that the Word of God has comforted you. Give glory to the Lord for His mercies. As this chapter ends, I encourage you to commit your ways unto the Lord, and watch Him come through for you: *"Commit thy way unto the Lord; trust also in him; and he shall bring it to pass"* (Psalm 37:5, KJV).

SUMMARY

Be encouraged, even when you go through bad experiences. Allow the Lord to comfort you through His Word. Be like David: encourage yourself in the Lord whenever you get into trouble. God is a way maker, and He is faithful to His Word. He will make a way for you.

PRAYER

*Lord, I choose to trust You through the challenging times.
Thank You, Lord, for reminding me how much You love me.
Lord, I thank You as You renew my strength. Thank You,
Lord, for helping me mount up with wings like eagles.
I run and do not get weary, and I walk and do not faint.
Lord, I ask that You remind me to encourage myself in the
Lord like David did when he faced the cares of life.
Lord, I ask that You give me the confidence to get professional
assistance with my life when I need it.*

DECLARATION OF FAITH

When I pass through the waters, You are with me. When I walk through the fire, the fire will not burn me.

ACTIVATION

- Ask the Lord to strengthen and comfort you in your time of trouble.
- Remind the Lord that He said He would make a way for you.
- Ask the Lord to show you whom you need to forgive and areas in your life that you need to surrender to Him.
- Ask the Lord to bring healing to your wounded heart.
- Thank the Lord for the opportunity to apply His Word to your life.
- Write down what you hear.

THIRTEEN
GOD IS A STORY CHANGER

"Every valley shall be filled.
And every mountain and hill brought low;
The crooked places shall be made straight.
And the rough ways smooth;
And all flesh shall see the salvation of God."
—**Luke 3:5–6, NKJV**—

God is a story changer. After reading the following accounts, may you receive grace to trust and believe God to change your stories in the name of Jesus. May God change them from unpleasant stories to beautiful ones for His glory.

God can level every mountain. Nothing is too hard for the Lord. He can handle a lawsuit, a prodigal son or daughter, an unsaved husband or wife, unemployment issues, and more. Seek help from God. He can change your story if you ask Him. He is the unquestionable God who can change things from evil to good.

God can change your ugly situation to a beautiful one. Your case may look like there is no way out, but God can change things for you, even overnight. When He is through with your case, everyone will see the goodness of the Lord in your life. Be encouraged. He remains faithful to His Word. He promised to give you joy in addition to your request: *"Hitherto have ye asked nothing in my name: ask, and ye shall receive, that your joy may be full"* (John 16:24, KJV). As you choose to trust the Lord, He will turn your mourning into dancing: *"Thou hast turned for me my mourning into dancing: thou hast put off my sackcloth and girded me with gladness"* (Psalm 30:11, KJV).

THE POWER OF PROPHECY AND PRAYER

During my first year in America, I attended the Christian Faith Center in Creed Moore. My pastor gave me a personal prophecy, saying, "Fear not concerning your career; I will walk and run with you." When I received this, I had an associate degree in nursing. Today, the prophecy that my late pastor gave has come to pass. I have a doctorate degree in psychotherapy. I agreed with my pastor and prayed for my career, and God answered. I give glory to the Lord for His faithfulness in my life. Maggie prophesied that I would write books, and she encouraged me to start writing. She said that it was just not right for me not to write. But I ignored her. Whenever she asked when I would start writing, I would inwardly laugh at her. Another good friend of mine also encouraged me to write. Still, I was not interested. But recently, my current pastor prophesied three times that I would start writing books. In addition, one of the church members predicted I would become an author.

I was comfortable with my life and was not looking to add any stress, such as researching and writing. However, with all the prophecies, I could no longer ignore that I needed to write. I revere the Word of God, which tells me, *"In the mouth of two or three witnesses shall every word be established"* (2 Corinthians 13:1, KJV). What is it that the Lord has called you to do for Him that you have ignored? The Lord is reminding you to do what He asked you; this is another chance from Him for you to get started. If you continue to disobey, the Lord has other people who will take your place. Obey the Lord: *"Behold, to obey is better than sacrifice, and to hearken than the fat of rams"* (1 Samuel 15:22, KJV).

STRENGTH FOR DIFFICULT TIMES

In life, there are often storms before the calm. While waiting and trusting God to change your story, things may get worse. Continue to trust the Lord to show up and change your situation. In previous chapters, we discussed the power in the Word, prayer, praise, and worship. As you reach out to the God who can change your story, keep using your weapons of warfare, and know that God answers prayer.

Although the fig tree shall not blossom, neither shall fruit be in the vines; the labor of the olive shall fail, and the fields shall yield no meat; the flock shall be cut off from the fold, and there shall be no herd in the stalls: Yet I will rejoice in the Lord, I will joy in the God of my salvation."

HABAKKUK 3:17–18, KJV

When you rejoice in the Lord during difficult times, this can trigger the God of salvation, the God who can change your story, to appear in the middle of your crisis:

The Lord God is my strength, and he will make my feet like hinds' feet, and he will make me to walk upon mine high places."

HABAKKUK 3:19, KJV

When you get to know God as your story changer, you can stand tall and bold, face difficult situations, and speak the Word of God over them. Your God, the story changer, will make all things possible for you: *"With God, all things are possible"* (Matthew 19:26, KJV).

You must invoke the power in the Word of God for your story changer to respond. Why? Because God responds to His Word. Jeremiah 1:12 says the Lord will hasten His Word to perform it.

Have confidence in God that He can change your story from impossible to possible. Boldly declare that nothing can separate you from God's love. Like Paul, you can confidently declare, *"For I am persuaded that neither death, nor life, nor angels, nor principalities, nor powers, nor things present, nor things to come, nor height, nor depth, nor any other creature, shall be able to separate us from the love of God, which is in Christ Jesus our Lord"* (Romans 8:38–39, KJV).

God is your story changer, and He will always show up for you when you call upon Him in times of trouble. He will turn your mourning to dancing, give you praise garments for the spirit of heaviness, and change your ugly stories into beautiful stories.[1]

GOD CHANGED THE STORY OF ANNA, THE PROPHETESS

Anna, the prophetess, was selfless. She believed that God would send the Lord Jesus to redeem Israel. She did not depart from the temple but served God with fasting and prayer night and day until Jesus was born. After Jesus was born, she was satisfied, and she glorified the Lord for sending Jesus to redeem His people:

Now there was one, Anna, a prophetess, the daughter of Phanuel, of the tribe of Asher. She was of a great age and had lived with a husband seven years from her virginity, and this woman was a widow of about eighty-four years,

> *who did not depart from the temple, but served God with fasting and prayers night and day. And coming in that instant she gave thanks to the Lord and spoke of Him to all those who looked for redemption in Jerusalem."*
>
> LUKE 2:36–38, NKJV

GOD CHANGED ESTHER'S STORY FROM A SLAVE GIRL TO A QUEEN

King Ahasuerus intended to show off his wife, Queen Vashti, to his visitors, subjects, and friends. Queen Vashti did not want to be paraded for people to see how beautiful she looked, so she refused:

> *But Queen Vashti refused to come at the king's commandment by his chamberlains: therefore, was the king very wroth, and his anger burned in him."*
>
> ESTHER 1:12, KJV

King Ahasuerus's advisors persuaded him to divorce Queen Vashti. As a result, he sought after a woman to replace Vashti:

> *Esther was taken unto king Ahasuerus into his house royal in the tenth month, which is the month Tebeth, in the seventh year of his reign. And the king loved Esther above all the women, and she obtained grace and favor in his sight more than all the virgins; so that he set the royal crown upon her head and made her queen instead of Vashti."*
>
> ESTHER 2:16–17, KJV

Esther had favor in the sight of God and King Ahasuerus. He loved Esther and made her the new queen. God changed the story of Esther from a slave girl to a queen.

GOD CHANGED JOASH'S STORY FROM ENDANGERED PRINCE TO A KING

When Athaliah found out that her son Ahaziah was dead, she killed all the royal seeds of the house of Judah. But God intervened on behalf of Judah. Jehoshabeath hid Joash, who later was made king:

> *But when Athaliah, the mother of Ahaziah, saw that her son was dead, she arose and destroyed all the seed royal of the house of Judah. But Jehoshabeath, the daughter of the king, took Joash the son of Ahaziah, and stole him from among the king's sons that were slain, and put him and his nurse in a bedchamber. So Jehoshabeath, the daughter of king Jehoram, the wife of Jehoiada the priest, (for she was the sister of Ahaziah), hid him from Athaliah, so that she slew him not. And he was with them hid in the house of God six years: and Athaliah reigned over the land."*
>
> 2 CHRONICLES 22:11–12, KJV

Be encouraged, child of God. The Lord keeps His Word and has confirmed His Word over and over again. He loves you. Listen to this: *"For thus saith the Lord; David shall never want a man to sit upon the throne of the house of Israel."* Jeremiah 33:17, KJV

God kept His promise to David. God changed Joash's death sentence in the hands of Athaliah to a life sentence in the hands of God:

> *Joash was seven years old when he began to reign, and he reigned forty years in Jerusalem. His mother's Name also*

was Zibiah of Beersheba. And Joash did that which was right in the sight of the Lord all the days of Jehoiada the priest."

2 CHRONICLES 24:2, KJV

GOD CHANGED THE STORY OF THE WOMAN OF CANAAN

God is merciful. When you understand how merciful He is, you will have the confidence to trust Him and keep asking for your miracle. A woman of Canaan asked Jesus to deliver her daughter, who was troubled by the devil. At first, Jesus ignored her, but then He replied that giving the children's bread to dogs was wrong. The woman was not offended. She pressed on, asking the Lord to have mercy on her, and worshiped Him. As a result, Jesus showed her mercy and changed her story. She received deliverance for her daughter:

> *But he answered and said, I am not sent but unto the lost sheep of the house of Israel. Then came she and worshiped him, saying, Lord, help me. But he answered and said, it is not meet to take the children's bread, and to cast it to dogs. And she said, Truth, Lord: yet the dogs eat of the crumbs which fall from their masters' table. Then Jesus answered and said unto her, O woman, great is thy faith be it unto thee even as thou wilt. And her daughter was made whole from that very hour."*

MATTHEW 15:24–28, KJV

Instead of being offended, the woman reminded Jesus that even the dogs eat from the crumbs on the floor. Her humility attracted favor from the Lord. Just as it was for the woman of Canaan, if you want

God to change your story, you must simply trust and ask Him for help, and He will change your story.

GOD CHANGED THE STORY OF THE TEN LEPERS

Jesus went to Jerusalem, and as He passed through Samaria and Galilee, Jesus met ten men who were lepers. The ten lepers asked Jesus to have mercy on them. Jesus heard their request and healed them:

> *And they lifted up their voices, and said, Jesus, Master, have mercy on us. And when he saw them, he said unto them, Go show yourselves unto the priests. And it came to pass, that, as they went, they were cleansed."*
>
> LUKE 17:13–14, KJV

Out of the ten lepers, only the one who was a stranger returned to thank God for his healing. It is imperative that when you ask God for help, and He helps you, that you return and give Him thanks so that you will be made completely whole:

> *And one of them, when he saw that he was healed, turned back, and with a loud voice glorified God. And fell down on his face at his feet, giving him thanks: and he was a Samaritan. And Jesus answering said, were there not ten cleansed? but where are the nine. There are not found that returned to give glory to God, save this stranger. And he said unto him, Arise, go thy way: thy faith hath made thee whole."*
>
> LUKE 17:15–19, KJV

GOD CHANGED THE STORY OF BLIND BARTIMAEUS

Blind Bartimaeus sat by the side of the road and begged. When he heard Jesus of Nazareth passing by, he cried loudly and asked Jesus to have mercy on him. The people around him were embarrassed and asked him to keep quiet, but he continued to cry and plead. Jesus opened Bartimaeus's eyes and changed his story:

> *And Jesus stood still and commanded him to be called. And they call the blind man, saying unto him, be of good comfort, rise; he calleth thee. And he, casting away his garment, rose, and came to Jesus. And Jesus answered and said unto him, what wilt thou that I should do unto thee? The blind man said unto him, Lord, that I might receive my sight. And Jesus said unto him, go thy way; thy faith hath made thee whole. And immediately he received his sight and followed Jesus in the way."*
>
> MARK 10:49–52, KJV

GOD CHANGED THE STORY OF A MAN FROM THE CROWD

One day, a man in the crowd asked Jesus to heal his son, whom the devil possessed. Because he was his only son, he was desperate. He explained to Jesus how the demon tormented his son. His situation was truly remarkable.

> *And as he was yet a coming, the devil threw him down, and tare him. And Jesus rebuked the unclean spirit, and healed the child, and delivered him again to his Father."*
>
> LUKE 9:42, KJV

Jesus had mercy and changed his story. Jesus healed his son. There is no situation too devastating for Jesus to make right and beautiful. Believe God to bless, keep, and heal your children as well.

GOD CHANGED THE STORY OF THE MADMAN AT GADARENES

When Jesus came to the region of Gadarenes during His time of ministry, a man possessed with an unclean spirit came out of the tombs to Him. He was completely bound and without hope. Look at how the Bible describes his hopeless situation:

> *Who had his dwelling among the tombs; and no man could bind him, no, not with chains. Because that he had been often bound with fetters and chains, and the chains had been plucked asunder by him, and the fetters broken in pieces: neither could any man tame him. And always, night and day, he was in the mountains, and in the tombs, crying, and cutting himself with stones."*
>
> MARK 5:3–5, KJV

When the man with the unclean spirit saw Jesus, he ran and worshiped Him. Jesus had compassion upon the man and delivered him from the unclean spirit: *"For he said unto him, come out of the man, thou unclean spirit"* (Mark 5:8, KJV).

Legions of spirits resided in the man; all the devils begged Jesus to send them into the swine, and He did. It was an astounding miracle to everyone who knew Him: *"And they come to Jesus, and see him that was possessed with the devil, and had the legion, sitting, and clothed, and in his right mind: and they were afraid"* (Mark 5:15, KJV).

Jesus delivered the madman from the legions of spirits that resided in him and changed his story.

SUMMARY

God is a story changer. As you trust and call upon Him in your time of trouble, He will answer you. Have faith in God; nothing is too difficult for Him to handle. When you take your problems to the Lord and ask Him to help, He will. Because of His faithful nature, God can change your negative stories to positive ones to glorify His name.

PRAYER

Father, I pray that You will change my story and make the people around me know You are God. I thank You for revealing Yourself as a story changer to me. Lord, I trust You to change my unpleasant stories to pleasant ones. Lord, I thank You for showing up for me in my difficult moments to change my situation over and over again. Lord, I thank You for not forsaking me in my challenging moments. And Lord, I ask that You give me the wisdom to reach out to You in my time of need as the God who can and will change my story when I pray.

DECLARATION OF FAITH

Thank You, Lord, for turning my mourning into dancing and giving me joy.

ACTIVATION

- Ask the Lord to show you areas where you need Him to change your stories. As He shows you each one, pray and release them to Him.

- Ask the Lord to come into those areas and do His will.
- Ask the Lord to visit you and change the negative stories in your life that you are not aware of, both spiritual and physical.
- Ask God to level every mountain. Name and release each problem to the Lord.
- Thank the Lord for solving every problem you released to Him.
- Write down what you hear.

FOURTEEN
THE GOD OF RESTORATION

"And I will restore to you the years that the locust hath eaten, the cankerworm, and the caterpillar, and the palmerworm, my great army which I sent among you. And ye shall eat in plenty, and be satisfied, and praise the name of the Lord your God, that hath dealt wondrously with you: and my people shall never be ashamed. And ye shall know that I am in the midst of Israel, and that I am the Lord your God, and none else: and my people shall never be ashamed."
—**Joel 2:25–27, KJV**—

The God who restores promises to meet you at the point of your need. For all the troubles, failures, broken hearts, sleepless nights, delays, denials, and disappointments you have encountered in life, I am here to remind you that the Lord can restore all that the enemy has stolen from you. Be intentional, and pray with persistence for restoration of what the devil took from you.

> *And from the days of John the Baptist until now, the kingdom of heaven suffereth violence, and the violent take it by force."*
>
> MATTHEW 11:12, KJV

God is the same yesterday, today, and forever. The Lord can repair, renew, and re-establish you. He can restore your current state and make it more glorious than your past state. Trust and believe that the Lord can restore to you all the things you have lost. I pray that as you draw close to the conclusion of this book, the Lord will help you believe in the God who restores:

> *Now the God of hope fill you with all joy and peace in believing, that ye may abound in hope, through the power of the Holy Ghost."*
>
> ROMANS 15:13, KJV

GOD WILL RESTORE WHAT THE ENEMY STEALS

For issues with physical or mental challenges, trust the Lord for wisdom, knowledge, and understanding as you follow and comply with your doctor's orders. As you look up to the Lord, He promises to restore your health:

> *For I will restore health unto thee, and I will heal thee of thy wounds, saith the Lord; because they called thee an Outcast, saying, this is Zion, whom no man seeketh after."*
>
> JEREMIAH 30:17, KJV

Have confidence in the Word of God. You should use the Word of God to your advantage. When you find yourself in a crisis or know that the enemy is taking advantage of you, ask God to reveal to you the most suitable words from the Bible that you can use to attack the enemy. For example:

 Men do not despise a thief if he steals to satisfy his soul when he is hungry. But if he be found, he shall restore sevenfold; he shall give all the substance of his house."

PROVERBS 6:31, KJV

Ask for a seven-fold return for what the enemy has stolen from you.

THE LORD RESTORED MY PRAYER PARTNER'S KNEES

In previous chapters, we discussed the importance of knowing God's Word and praying for God's will. I encourage you to use wisdom as you pray. The Holy Spirit will direct you as you yield to Him. For example, Maggie called me one day and asked that I pray for her. She said one of her friends was preparing for a surgical bilateral knee replacement. I thought, *Okay? And what has that got to do with your knees?* Then she told me she had pain in both her knees, and she feared she might need bilateral knee replacement.

I told my prayer partner we had many things to pray about, but there was one thing she needed to do first. I asked her to start watching what she ate. She should start eating more nutritious meals, drink water instead of consuming drinks with added sugar, and reduce her carbohydrate intake. We laughed and decided to watch what we both ate. She was not angry at my recommendation; she followed the directions and noticed positive improvements. The pain in her knees disappeared after a couple of months.

Note how the enemy tried to instill fear into my prayer partner's mind. The enemy used fear to open the door and prepare her to embrace the idea of knee replacement surgery. But God intervened. Because she did what I asked her to do, she had no pain in her limbs or knees, and she praised God. As I am authoring this book, the knee pain has not returned. To God be all the glory!

Please consult your doctor for any advice if you experience pain in your knees. Also, talk to your nutritionist before you start any diet plan.

GOD GAVE JOB TWICE AS MUCH AS HE HAD BEFORE

As you encounter difficulties in life, it is important to use the Word of God as a reference point. Not every tough time you encounter in life is your fault, especially if you are a child of God. The Bible tells us in Job 1:1–8 that Job was perfect, upright, feared God, and eschewed evil. Job had seven sons and three daughters. He had seven thousand sheep, three thousand camels, five hundred yoke of oxen, five hundred donkeys, and a very great household. Job was the greatest man in the east. He offered burnt offerings on behalf of his children to account for any sins and curses against God in their hearts.

The Bible states that one day, the sons of God came to present themselves before the Lord, and Satan came among them. The Lord decided on that day to brag about His servant Job. Satan's reply to the Lord was that Job feared God because of the blessings he had obtained from the Lord. Satan said to God that Job would curse God if He removed His blessings from the life of Job. As a result of the dialogue between God and Satan, God permitted Satan to take away all that Job had:

 And the Lord said unto Satan, Hast thou considered my servant Job, that there is none like him in the earth, a

perfect and an upright man, one that feareth God, and escheweth evil. Then Satan answered the Lord, and said, Doth Job fear God for nought. Hast not thou made a hedge about him, and about his house, and about all that he hath on every side? thou hast blessed the work of his hands, and his substance is increased in the land. But put forth thine hand now, and touch all that he hath, and he will curse thee to thy face. And the Lord said unto Satan, Behold, all that he hath is in thy power; only upon himself put not forth thine hand. So, Satan went forth from the presence of the Lord."

JOB 1:8–12, KJV

Satan left the presence of the Lord and tormented Job to his satisfaction. He took away everything that Job had. But Job knew God—He was a God that restores. Instead of being bitter, Job praised and worshiped the God that can restore:

Then Job arose, and rent his mantle, and shaved his head, and fell down upon the ground, and worshiped. And said, Naked came I out of my mother's womb, and naked shall I return thither: the Lord gave, and the Lord hath taken away; blessed be the name of the Lord. In all this Job sinned not, nor charged God foolishly."

JOB 1:20–22, KJV

God saw Job's humility and had mercy upon him. The Lord restored to Job all that the enemy took away. God blessed Job's latter years and gave Job twice as much as he had before:

And the Lord turned the captivity of Job, when he prayed for his friends: also, the Lord gave Job twice as much as he

had before. Then came there unto him all his brethren, and all his sisters, and all they that had been of his acquaintance before and did eat bread with him in his house: and they bemoaned him and comforted him over all the evil that the Lord had brought upon him: every man also gave him a piece of money, and everyone an earring of gold. So, the Lord blessed the latter end of Job more than his beginning: for he had fourteen thousand sheep, and six thousand camels, and a thousand yoke of oxen, and a thousand she asses. He also had seven sons and three daughters. And he called the name of the first, Jemima; and the name of the second, Kezia; and the name of the third, Kerenhappuch. And in all the land were no women found so fair as the daughters of Job: and their father gave them inheritance among their brethren. After this lived Job a hundred and forty years, and saw his sons, and his sons' sons, even four generations. So, Job died, being old and full of days."

JOB 42:10–17, KJV

God did it for Job, and He will do it for you. According to Psalm 51:12 (KJV), the Lord will restore to you the joy of your salvation and uphold you with His Spirit.

GLORIFY GOD FOR YOUR RESTORATION

God is still in the business of restoration. When God restores to you what the enemy had destroyed, be careful to give Him all the glory. As indicated in Isaiah 42:8 (KJV), He will not share His glory.

The children of Israel knew that they should always return all the glory to the Lord, so when the Lord freed Israel from their bondage and brought them back to Zion, they praised God. When the prophecy was fulfilled, the children of Israel were careful to glorify the Lord for keeping His promises:

When the Lord turned again the captivity of Zion, we were like them that dream. Then was our mouth filled with laughter, and our tongue with singing then said they among the heathen, The Lord hath done great things for them. The Lord hath done great things for us; whereof we are glad."

PSALM 126:1–3, KJV

GOD BLESSED RUTH AND NAOMI WITH OBED

As recorded in Ruth 1:1–14, there was a famine in the land of Israel. Elimelech, his wife Naomi, and their two sons, Mahlon and Chilion, relocated to the country of Moab. Elimelech died. The two sons got married to Orpah and Ruth, and after living in Moab ten years, Mahlon and Chilion also died. Naomi decided to return to Israel because she heard that the Lord had visited His people and given them bread. Naomi persuaded Orpah to go back to her parents, but Ruth decided to follow Naomi back to Israel. While in Israel, Boaz married Ruth, and God blessed Ruth and Boaz with a son:

So, Boaz took Ruth, and she was his wife: and when he went in unto her, the Lord gave her conception, and she bare a son. And the women said unto Naomi, Blessed be the Lord, which hath not left thee this day without a kinsman, that his name may be famous in Israel. And he shall be unto thee a restorer of thy life, and a nourisher of thine old age: for thy daughter in law, which loveth thee, which is better to thee than seven sons, hath born him. And Naomi took the child, and laid it in her bosom, and became nurse unto it. And the women her neighbors gave it a name, saying, there

is a son born to Naomi; and they called his name Obed: he is the father of Jesse, the father of David."

RUTH 4:13–17, KJV

Who would have known that Jesus Christ, the son of David, would come from a background of such trauma, difficulties, and challenges? But the Lord is the God who restores: *"The book of the generation of Jesus Christ, the son of David, the son of Abraham"* (Matthew 1:1, KJV).

DELIVERANCE FOR THE HOUSE OF JACOB

After Joseph gave Pharaoh the interpretation of his dreams, God gave Joseph favor in the sight of Pharaoh. Joseph's words became as precious as gold to Pharaoh.

God restored, repaired, renewed, and re-established Joseph as He has promised from the beginning of time:

> *And I will strengthen the house of Judah, and I will save the house of Joseph, and I will bring them again to place them; for I have mercy upon them: and they shall be as though I had not cast them off: for I am the Lord their God and will hear them."*

ZECHARIAH 10:6, KJV

The Lord promised the children of Israel that He will be to them a God who restores, and He has kept His Word to His people:

> *I will open rivers in high places, and fountains in the midst of the valleys: I will make the wilderness a pool of water, and the dry land springs of water. I will plant in the wilderness the cedar, the shittah tree, and the myrtle, and*

the oil tree; I will set in the desert the fir tree, and the pine, and the box tree together. That they may see, and know, and consider, and understand together, that the hand of the Lord hath done this, and the Holy One of Israel hath created it."

ISAIAH 41:18–20, KJV

JESUS RESTORED SIGHT TO THE BLIND MAN

At Bethsaida, Jesus met a blind man, and the people persuaded Him to heal him. Jesus had compassion for the blind man:

And he took the blind man by the hand and led him out of the town; when he had spit on his eyes and put his hands upon him, he asked him if he saw ought. And he looked up and said, I see men as trees, walking. After that he put his hands again upon his eyes and made him look up: and he was restored and saw every man clearly."

MARK 8:23–25, KJV

Why did Jesus take the blind man to a different location to perform the healing? We may never know. We should be sensitive to the leading of the Holy Spirit.

As you draw close to the end of this chapter, may the Lord bless you with a double portion for all that the enemy took from you. May He give you everlasting joy for confusion, just as He promised through the prophet Isaiah: *"For your shame, ye shall have double; and for confusion, they shall rejoice in their portion: therefore, in their land, they shall possess the double: everlasting joy shall be unto them"* (Isaiah 61:7, KJV).

Wait on the God of restoration; He can meet you at the point of any need and bring restoration, no matter how impossible your situation may seem. Continue to pray and believe God to answer your prayer just as Elias did:

Elias was a man subject to like passions as we are, and he prayed earnestly that it might not rain: And it rained not on the earth by the space of three years and six months. And he prayed again, and heaven gave rain, and the earth brought forth her fruit."

JAMES 5:17–18, KJV

SUMMARY

We serve a God who keeps His Word. He is a faithful God. He promised He will restore to you everything that you lost. Call upon Him when you find yourself in challenging situations. Trust and believe Him, and know that He will not let you down. He is the God who restores.

PRAYER

Lord, I call upon You to restore all that the enemy has stolen from me. Lord, You promised to answer my prayer, and I believe You. Lord, I ask that You fill me with all joy and peace in believing that I may abound in hope through the power of the Holy Ghost. And I thank You for manifesting Your restoration power in my life. According to Your words, I take back everything the enemy took from me. In the name of Jesus, I pray. Amen.

DECLARATION OF FAITH

Lord, I declare that the enemy is a thief, and according to your words, I take back everything that the enemy has stolen: *"And from the days of John the Baptist until now, the kingdom of heaven suffereth violence, and the violent take it by force"* (Matthew 11:12, KJV).

ACTIVATION

- Ask the Lord to show you areas in your life that need restoration. Remind the Lord of His promise to restore all that the enemy stole from you.
- Ask the Lord to restore your soul and lead you to the path of righteousness.
- Thank the Lord for restoring the joy of your salvation and upholding you with His Spirit.
- Take time in prayer, and ask the Lord to show you what you need to do for the Lord to restore what the enemy took from you.
- Ask the Lord to teach you how to keep what the Lord has restored.
- Thank the Lord for keeping His promise of restoring all that the enemy has stolen from you.
- Write down what you hear.

FIFTEEN
THE GOD OF THE ELEVENTH HOUR

> *"Lord, remember me when You come into Your kingdom, and Jesus said to him, assuredly, I say to you, today you will be with Me in Paradise."*
> **—Luke 23:43, NKJV—**

The eleventh hour is the hour when everything is about to come to an end and all seems lost. For the thief on the cross, in Luke 23:43, his eleventh hour became a glorious turnaround. He met Jesus, his sins were forgiven, and he transitioned to Heaven.

The eleventh hour can be described as the hour of crisis, an hour when supernatural intervention is needed. The eleventh hour is the time when the reality of life unfolds and we need God to show up.

What happens when the God of the eleventh hour visits you? He answers your prayer, brings help when all hope is gone, and surprises everyone. When all hope is gone, and you have tried everything to make things happen to no avail, then the God of the eleventh hour, the incomprehensible God, steps in and majestically takes the battle to a higher and more complicated level, where He becomes the only one qualified to get the glory.

If this is your story, and you need the God of the eleventh hour to show up, be encouraged. The Lord is about to surprise you. He will not leave you. He promises, *"I will never leave thee, nor forsake thee"* (Hebrews 13:5, KJV). He cannot deny Himself: *"If we believe not, yet he abides faithful: he cannot deny himself"* (2 Timothy 2:13, KJV).

BILATERAL BLOCKED FALLOPIAN TUBES

As a newly married woman who wanted to have children, my friend Theresa received a diagnosis from her gynecologist of bilateral blocked fallopian tubes. Instead of becoming discouraged, she went into a warfare mode. She prayed, praised, fasted, and stayed in the Word of God. The God of the eleventh hour showed up. Even though the doctor said she had two blocked fallopian tubes, she got pregnant and delivered a girl. Theresa continued to trust God, and three more children came out of those blocked fallopian tubes. In the end, she gave birth to two girls and two boys. She prayed and God answered:

In my distress I called upon the Lord, and cried unto my God: he heard my voice out of his temple, and my cry came before him, even into his ears."

PSALM 18:6, KJV

God also blessed Theresa with the anointing of praying for women who seek the fruit of the womb. When she prays and agrees with these women, they get pregnant with miracle babies. God can do the same for you; He can make your barren places fruitful.

WORKERS IN THE VINEYARD

In Matthew 20, Jesus told a parable to describe the God of the eleventh hour. A householder went out early in the morning to hire laborers for his vineyard. He decided to pay the laborers a penny a day for their services. They signed the contract, and he put them to work. He went out about the third hour, saw others standing idle in the marketplace, and hired them. Again, he went out about the sixth and ninth hours and did likewise. Finally, the householder went and persuaded the last set of workers to come work for him at the eleventh hour.

At the end of the workday, the vineyard's owner paid all the workers one penny each, from the last to the first. The laborers who started working earlier than the eleventh hour murmured against the vineyard's owner. He answered them:

> *Take what is yours and go your way. I wish to give to this last man the same as to you. Is it not lawful for me to do what I wish with my own things? Or is your eye evil because I am good? So, the last will be first, and the first last. For many are called, but few chosen."*
>
> MATTHEW 20:14–16, NKJV

The God of the eleventh hour will meet you where you are. He will settle you, visit with you, and restore the time you have lost.

JEHOVAH JIREH, GOD OF THE ELEVENTH HOUR

As recorded in Genesis 22:1–11, God asked Abraham to take his only and beloved son, Isaac, to the land of Moriah and offer him there for a burnt offering upon one of the mountains. Abraham obeyed. He rose early in the morning, saddled his donkeys, and took two of his young men with him, Isaac, and the wood for the burnt offering. It was a three-day journey. When they arrived, Abraham asked the young men who accompanied him to wait with the donkeys so that he and Isaac could go and worship. Abraham took the wood for the burnt offering and laid it upon Isaac; he took the fire and a knife, and they went together. Isaac asked his father, "Where is the lamb for a burnt offering?" Abraham said, "My son, God will provide Himself a lamb."

They continued until they came to the place God had told him of. Abraham built an altar, laid the wood, bound Isaac, and laid him on the altar upon the wood. When Abraham reached out to get the knife to slay Isaac, the angel of the Lord called out and stopped him:

> *And he said, lay not thine hand upon the lad, neither do thou anything unto him: for now, I know that thou fearest God, seeing thou hast not withheld thy son, thine only son from me. And Abraham lifted up his eyes, and looked, and behold behind him a ram caught in a thicket by his horns: and Abraham went and took the ram and offered him up for a burnt offering in the stead of his son. And Abraham called the name of that place Jehovah Jireh: as it is said to this day, In the mount of the Lord it shall be seen."*
>
> GENESIS 22:1–11, KJV

The God of the eleventh hour provided a ram for the sacrifice in place of Isaac.

THE PRICE FOR OBEDIENCE

The Lord was pleased with Abraham after he agreed to offer his only son as a sacrifice. Abraham heard a voice from Heaven saying:

> *By myself have I sworn, saith the Lord, for because thou hast done this thing, and hast not withheld thy son, thine only son. That in blessing I will bless thee, and in multiplying I will multiply thy seed as the stars of the heaven, and as the sand which is upon the seashore; and thy seed shall possess the gate of his enemies. And in thy seed shall all the nations of the earth be blessed; because thou hast obeyed my voice."*
>
> GENESIS 22:16–18, KJV

When you obey Him, the God of the eleventh hour will multiply your blessings.

THE BORROWED AX

The sons of the prophets decided to build themselves a house in Jordan. Elisha permitted them to build the house. As they cut down the wood, the ax head fell into the water. The sons of the prophet were disturbed because they had borrowed the ax. But a miracle happened.

Elisha helped the men recover it at the eleventh hour:

> *And the man of God said, where fell it? And he showed him the place. And he cut down a stick and cast it in thither;*

and the iron did swim. Therefore, said he, take it up to thee. And he put out his hand and took it."

2 KINGS 6:6–7, KJV

Elisha prayed, and the God of the eleventh hour answered and brought out the ax from the water.

GOD OF THE ELEVENTH HOUR SAVES ISRAEL

The king of Syria disclosed to his servants that he would attack Israel at a particular location. God revealed his intentions to Elisha, the prophet. Elisha notified the king of Israel, who listened to Elisha and avoided the said location.

The king of Syria was troubled and wondered who was revealing his secrets to the Israelites. One of his servants told him that Elisha was the revealer of his secret. The king of Syria sent horses, chariots, and a great host by night and surrounded the city where Elisha was. In the morning, Elisha's servant saw the army of Syria and was afraid, but Elisha asked him not to be frightened. He prayed and smote the Syrians with blindness:

And he answered, Fear not: for they that be with us are more than they that be with them. And Elisha prayed, and said, Lord, I pray thee, open his eyes, that he may see. And the Lord opened the eyes of the young man; and he saw: and behold, the mountain was full of horses and chariots of fire round about Elisha. And when they came down to him, Elisha prayed unto the Lord, and said, smite these people, I pray thee, with blindness. And he smote them with blindness according to the word of Elisha."

2 KINGS 6:16–18, KJV

Elisha blinded and took the Syrian army to Samaria, and then he prayed that the Lord should open their eyes. Elisha asked the king of Israel to feed the Syrian army and send them back to their master:

> *And he prepared great provision for them: and when they had eaten and drunk, he sent them away, and they went to their master. So, the bands of Syria came no more into the land of Israel."*
>
> 2 KINGS 6:23, KJV

The God of the eleventh hour saved Elisha and the Israelites from the armed army.

GRATITUDE CAN TRIGGER THE GOD OF THE ELEVENTH HOUR

In chapter 2, you read about how Maggie's surgical site looked like wet bread. Although things were not looking good, we praised God in advance for our victory. We brought in gratitude to the battlefield. As we waited, we prayed, praised, worshiped, and reminded God of His promise for us. The God of the eleventh hour intervened and healed Maggie's wound.

Show gratitude to God in everything. The enemy magnifies little problems and wants to convince you that your life is over. The enemy tries to cover your view, and he does not want you to see the goodness of God in your life. You have to be intentional with your gratitude, especially to the Lord. Take some time alone, with a loved one, or with friends. Remove the blindfold the enemy has placed over your spiritual eyes, covering your eyes from God's beautiful world. Instead of focusing on the enemy's lies, count your blessings, call them by name, get a journal, and write. You will be amazed at what the Lord has done, is doing, and will continue to do in your life. If you can breathe, walk, eat, and so on, you must show gratitude to your Maker.

I encourage you to trust the God of the eleventh hour. He is the creator of all things:

Have you not known? Have you not heard? The everlasting God, the Lord, The Creator of the ends of the earth, neither faints nor is weary. His understanding is unsearchable. He gives power to the weak, and to those who have no might He increases strength. Even the youths shall faint and be weary, And the young men shall utterly fall. But those who wait on the Lord shall renew their strength; They shall mount up with wings like eagles. They shall run and not be weary. They shall walk and not faint."

ISAIAH 40:28–31, NKJV

God's ways are different from our ways. God is the unquestionable One. We must familiarize ourselves with His words and His ways. He has mercy upon whom He will, and there is no unrighteousness with Him. King David encountered many troubles; each time he was troubled, he called upon the God of his eleventh hour. God delighted in answering his prayers:

I will call upon the Lord, who is worthy to be praised: so, shall I be saved from mine enemies. The sorrows of death compassed me, and the floods of ungodly men made me afraid. The sorrows of hell compassed me about: the snares of death prevented me. In my distress, I called upon the Lord and cried unto my God: he heard my voice out of his temple, and my cry came before him, even into his ears."

PSALM 18:3–6, KJV

God loved David so much because even when David did what was evil in the sight of God, David would run to the Lord: *"And David said unto Gad, I am in a great strait: let us fall now into the hand of the Lord; for his mercies are great: and let me not fall into the hand of man"* (2 Samuel 24:14, KJV).

God called David a man after His heart, saying, *"I have found David, the son of Jesse, a man after mine own heart"* (Psalm 18:22, KJV).

I encourage you to remember to return all the glory to the Lord each time He meets you at the point of your need, just like David did. When he experienced God's great help, he proclaimed, *"The Lord lives; and blessed be my rock; and let the God of my salvation be exalted"* (Psalm 18:22, KJV).

Dear reader, even when you go through tough times, remember to let the words out of your mouth glorify God. May you receive access to the God of the eleventh hour when you need help.

SUMMARY

As you end this book, expect to receive your supernatural encounter with the Lord. And when you do, be careful to give Him all the glory.

Remember, He is a miracle worker, willing to perform a miracle for you if you ask Him. The Word of God explains the ways of God and outlines the rules and regulations we must follow and fulfill to please God. For this reason, you must familiarize yourself with the Bible.

PRAYER

Lord, I choose to call upon You at the hour of my crisis.
You are merciful and gracious, and I thank You, Lord, for
always hearing my prayer. Lord, help me to run to You when I find

myself in trouble instead of running away from You. I pray that even when I go through hard times, I will remember to let the words that come out of my mouth glorify You.

DECLARATION OF FAITH

Thank You, Lord, for meeting me at the point of my need.

ACTIVATION

- Take some time to call on the Lord and invite Him into your eleventh-hour situations.
- Remind the Lord of His promise to not leave you in your time of trouble.
- Ask the Lord to show you what to do when faced with challenging moments.
- Ask the Lord to give you the grace to praise and worship Him in difficult times.
- Ask the Lord to teach you how to run to Him when you are in trouble instead of running away from Him.
- Thank the God of your eleventh hour and remind Him that He is faithful.
- Write down what you hear.

SIXTEEN
FINAL THOUGHTS

I bless the Lord for the privilege to share His Word with you. I do not take this opportunity for granted. I want to take this moment to give thanks to the Lord. I give God all the glory for allowing me to author this book. Here is my thank-you prayer:

> *Bless the Lord, O my soul: and all that is within me, bless his holy name. Bless the Lord, O my soul, and forget not all his benefits. Who forgives all thine iniquities, who heals all thy diseases. Who redeems thy life from destruction, who crowns thee with lovingkindness and tender mercies. Who satisfies thy mouth with good things; so that thy youth is renewed like the eagle's."*
>
> PSALM 103:1–5, NKJV

I will continue to allow God to comfort His children through me. Father, I acknowledge You to be the Lord, and I praise You with all my heart: *"Now to Him who is able to do exceedingly abundantly above all that we ask or think, according to the power that works in us, to*

Him be glory in the church by Christ Jesus to all generations, forever and ever. Amen" (Ephesians 3:20–21, NKJV).

As a gentle reminder of the truths we have covered in this book, read God's Word and pray according to God's will. Pay your vow if you make one. The peace of God is your portion in life. God has not given you the spirit of fear but of power, love, and a sound mind. Call upon the Lord in your time of trouble, and He will deliver you. God is a story changer, a restorer, and the God of the eleventh hour. In His Word and in your life, you will find Him to be your God of the eleventh hour. He is faithful, and He will never fail you.

Thank you to my readers. May the Lord turn all your life challenges to an eleventh hour blessing. And remember that according to Philippians 4:13, we can do all things through Christ who strengthens us.

Coming Soon
A Blessing to Generations

NOTES

2. MIRACLE WORKING GOD

1. The Hope Christian Church located at 6251 Ammendale Road, Beltsville, MD 20705.

6. PRAYING FOR THE WILL OF GOD

1. See Ephesians 5:17, KJV.

9. FINDING PEACE IN ANY SITUATION

1. "Peaceful Definition & Meaning," Merriam-Webster, accessed October 17, 2023, https://www.merriam-webster.com/dictionary/peaceful.

10. WHAT IS FEAR?

1. "Fear Definition & Meaning," Merriam-Webster, accessed October 17, 2023, https://www.merriam-webster.com/dictionary/fear.
2. Walter Bradford Cannon (October 19, 1871 – October 1, 1945) was an American physiologist, professor and chairman of the Department of Physiology at Harvard Medical School.
3. Gozhenko, A; Gurkalova, I.P.; Zukow, W; Kwasnik, Z (2009). PATHOLOGY – Theory. Medical Student's Library. Radom. pp. 270–275.

11. DELIVERANCE FROM THE ENEMY

1. See Obadiah 1:17, KJV.

13. GOD IS A STORY CHANGER

1. See Isaiah 61:3.

ACKNOWLEDGMENTS

I give all the glory to God the Father, God the Son, and God the Holy Spirit. Lord, because of your love, writing this book was possible.

To Maggie, my friend and prayer partner, thank you so much for your spiritual support. You stated, "This shall not remain under the carpet. The Lord must be glorified in your life." Maggie, your prophecy came to pass. You are a real prophet. God bless you mightily in Jesus's name. Amen.

ABOUT THE AUTHOR

Dr. Eno Oton, a Christian counselor, lives in Maryland and is a psychotherapist in a counseling firm. She is a trained nurse-midwife who has worked for over thirty years as a registered nurse. By the grace of God, she went back to school for her doctorate to acquire knowledge so that she could practice her profession based on empirical evidence and make decisions concerning the care of her clients based on well-informed research data, which equals best practices.

Dr. Eno loves the Lord and loves to read the Word. She loves to take walks in the morning and listen to the Word or to gospel music. She is originally from Nigeria and loves to cook Nigerian food for friends and family. In addition to cooking, she also loves to travel.

Dr. Eno is an encourager and loves to encourage people outside of her profession. She wrote this book to reach everyone the Lord would allow her to touch with encouraging words. Anyone who is troubled, be encouraged. Your God is working for you behind the scenes; to God be the glory for the power of your courageous faith.

Made in the USA
Columbia, SC
27 November 2024

47171018R10107